Mountaineering Women

Mountaineering Women

STORIES BY EARLY CLIMBERS

Edited, with an Introduction, by **David Mazel**

Texas A&M University Press
College Station

The paper used in this book meets the minimum requirements
of the American National Standard for Permanence
of Paper for Printed Library Materials, Z39.48-1984.
Binding materials have been chosen for durability.
∞

Library of Congress Cataloging-in-Publication Data
Moutaineering women : stories by early climbers / edited, with an
    introduction, by David Mazel.
        p.   cm.
    Includes bibliographical references (p.).
    ISBN 0-89096-616-8. — ISBN 0-89096-617-6 (pbk.)
    1. Women mountaineers—Case studies. 2. Women mountaineers—
History. I. Mazel, David.
    GV199.M68   1994
    796.5'22'0922—dc20
    [B]   94-11260
                                                                            CIP

Acknowledgment is gratefully made for permission to reprint the following material:

Lily Bristow's "A Real Snorker," reprinted courtesy of *The Alpine Jour-
nal* and the Alpine Club.
"A Secret, Cherished History" from Dorothy Pilley's *Climbing Days* (Lon-
don: Chatto & Windus, 1989), reprinted courtesy of Chatto & Windus.
"Alone at Last" from Nea Morin's *A Woman's Reach: Mountaineering
Memories* (New York: Dodd, Mead, 1969). Copyright © Nea Morin 1969.
"I Was the One on Trial" from Gwen Moffat's *Space Below My Feet*
(London: Hodder and Stoughton, 1961). Reprinted courtesy of Gwen
Moffat.
"The Whole Splendour of Our Situation" from Elizabeth Stark and
Monica Jackson, *Tents in the Clouds: The First Women's Himalayan Expedi-
tion* (London: Travel Book Club, 1957), reprinted courtesy of Methuen
London.

To Jeannine Blanche Ward Mazel

Contents

Illustrations

Preface

Although women have been climbing mountains for two centuries, the first English-language history of their achievements appeared just twenty years ago. The topic has not really been treated adequately since then, and as yet there has been no historical anthology such as this one. While this book is no substitute for a thorough and up-to-date study of the long and varied history of women's climbing, I hope it will prompt and assist the sort of treatment the subject deserves.

I could not have edited this collection alone. First of all, I am indebted to several climbers whom I have never met but whose writing clarified the need for a collection such as this one: Rosie Andrews, Arlene Blum, Sallie Greenwood, Alison Osius, Janet Robertson, Susan Rogers, and Rachel da Silva. They raised the issues that prompted me to undertake this project in the first place. In fact, if there is any single point of origin to which this book can be traced, it is a comment made by Rogers in the 1987 Special Women's Issue of *Climbing*: "That the history of women climbers is silent . . . is no surprise. It duplicates the pre-feminist history of people—men—in any activity outside the home. As with all women's studies, women have to be sought after, rediscovered. . . ."

Second, anyone who takes mountaineering literature seriously owes a debt to Jill Neate, author of the pioneering bibliography *Mountaineering and Its Literature* (1979). Her follow-up *Mountaineering Literature* (1983), which expanded the original list to more than thirty-four hundred titles, is by far the best reference work on the subject, and was the starting point of my own research. Neate died in the spring of 1993, while hiking in England's Lake District.

Among the many people who helped me more directly, I wish to thank Dana Nelson, Robin Roberts, Phyllis Thompson, Joanna Barszewska Marshall, Nancy Dixon, Chris Healy, John Fischer, and Catherine Williamson; Roberta Ruiz, Marjo Arseneau, and the staff of Louisiana State University's Troy H. Middleton Library; Faye Phillips, Bob Martin, Elaine Smyth, and the staff of Hill Memorial Library; the Text Processing Center of LSU's College of Arts and Sciences; Yvette Vaucher, Gwen Moffat, George Meyers, Michael Chessler, and Heinke Forfota; Johanna Merz of the Alpine Journal, François Bonnet of Les Alpes, Alison Osius of Climbing, and George Bracksieck of Rock and Ice; Franc de la Vega of the American Alpine Club, Shirley Angell of the Pinnacle Club, and Kevin Lohka of the Alpine Club of Canada; Jennifer Brathovde of the Library of Congress, Bob Lawford of the Alpine Club Library, and Alex Huculak of the Whyte Museum of the Canadian Rockies; and finally, the servers and chefs at Louie's Cafe in Baton Rouge.

Mountaineering Women

Introduction

Perhaps we got tired of being taken in hand by men climbers. . . . As in other walks of life, women wanted to find their own feet: it was very splendid for some women to be always able to borrow crutches in the form of a man's help, and a man's rope, but it is even better to find that we have feet of our own.

—Emily Kelly

I owe a supreme debt of gratitude to the mountains for knocking from me the shackles of conventionality.

—Elizabeth Le Blond

Women have been climbing high mountains for a long time, since at least 1808, when a French servant named Marie Paradis reached the 15,771-foot summit of Mont Blanc.[1] For almost as long, their climbing has brought them into close contact and cooperation as well as bitter conflict with men. In 1838, during a visit to the Pyrenees, Anne Lister climbed an imposing, 10,820-foot peak called the Vignemale, becoming the first woman on record to arouse the antagonism of a male climber by beating him out of a coveted first ascent. She had made the climb with a local guide named Cazaux; four days later, Cazaux repeated the climb with another visitor, the Prince of Moscowa. Apparently eager to please such a wealthy client, Cazaux told him Lister had not climbed all the way to Vignemale's summit and that the prince should, thus, receive credit for the first amateur ascent. Lister wrote in her diary that she was "annoyed" by this perfidy, and she vowed she "would not pay Cazaux till this was cleared. Either I had gone to the top or I had not, and if I had it should be acknowledged." She consulted a lawyer, and Cazaux was asked to sign an affidavit indicating that

Lister had in fact been first to the top. He signed, later admitting that Lister not only had made the climb but "got up very well too."[2] The incident thus ended satisfactorily, but it would hardly be the last time that men would conspire to undercut the significance of a woman's accomplishments.

The first woman to climb extensively in the Alps—and to be widely acknowledged as a serious alpinist—was the Frenchwoman Henriette d'Angeville. Born in 1794 in the later turmoils of the French Revolution, d'Angeville grew up in the countryside near Bugey, an elevated region where she enjoyed taking long hikes in the hills and from which, on a clear day, she could see the Alps in the distance. As an adult she spent her summers in Geneva, mixing in the best society but not giving up her long, strenuous walks. It was on one of these hikes that she first became inflamed with the idea of climbing Mont Blanc, the highest point in Europe and the mountain whose first ascent, in 1786, had inaugurated the sport of alpinism. Seeing the mountain resplendent with fresh snow, she was transported "into a state that even today I can hardly understand or explain; my heart beat violently, my breath became short, profound sighs escaped from my breast. I felt a desire to climb it so ardent that it gave movement even to my feet."[3] When she made her mountaineering ambition public, so many people opposed her that it seemed her biggest obstacle would be to overcome public opinion. The number of well-meaning acquaintances seeking to dissuade her grew so great that for a time she had to stop receiving visitors altogether. Her doctor also tried to talk her out of it, and the local priest was reluctant to bless the proposed climb because both "guides and priest would be blamed if some misfortune occurs."

In Chamonix, at the base of the mountain itself, d'Angeville had difficulty recruiting guides for the expedition, and not only because she was a woman—the memory of a disastrous 1820 expedition in which three climbers had died was still fresh enough to make the guides leery of taking what they saw as an unprecedented risk. Finally, however, she secured the services of the well-respected Joseph-Marie Couttet and began preparing for the ascent. She made out her will, then made practice climbs to the Talefre Glacier and to 8,106-foot Mont Joli— experiences which reinforced her confidence that she had what it took for the much more difficult ascent of Mont Blanc.

Once finally on the mountain itself, d'Angeville found that her experience served her well. She excelled particularly on the rock cliffs known as the Rochers Rouges, climbing them, the guides said afterward, with as much facility as any man. Near the top she was almost defeated by acute altitude sickness, a temporary but extremely debilitating condition that afflicts even the strongest mountaineers when they climb high without allowing sufficient time to acclimatize. Once on the summit, fortunately, she recovered quickly. "As soon as I was on top," she wrote later, "the resurrection was immediate. I recovered all my strength at once . . . and all my intellectual power, which enabled me to enjoy that magnificent scene in all its grandeur!"[4]

D'Angeville was conscious of the importance of her ascent and sought to ensure that it would signify clearly her own strength and capability as a woman mountaineer. Thus when her guides had suggested she combine her climbing party with two others then in Chamonix—each composed entirely of men—she insisted upon traveling separately. She similarly refused the offer of a mule to conduct her up and down the lower slopes of the peak, noting that, since men typically made the entire ascent under their own power, she would do no less herself. The same gender consciousness informs the account of the climb she wrote a year afterward. She noted, for example, that "the manner of seeing and of feeling of women sometimes differs from that of men, and Mont Blanc, when I went there, had not yet been visited by any woman able to give an account of her impressions"—a fact that emphasized the pioneering nature of both her ascent and the accounts she wrote of it. And of all the advice she received on how best to write her story, she valued most highly this: "Don't take anyone's advice, especially a man's, because it is necessary that this narration bear the feminine character."[5]

Why did she make the climb? One historian suggests that d'Angeville, who never married, "loved Mont Blanc because she had nothing else to love" and had "a morbid passion for self-advertisement" fueled by an insane jealousy of her famous contemporary, George Sand.[6] D'Angeville's own writings, however, suggest that she possessed the romantic passion for mountains so typical of her time, and her subsequent career proves that she was no mere publicity seeker, but rather a genuine alpinist, for she went on to make a total of twenty-one climbs—the final one, an ascent of the 10,250-foot Oldenhorn, at the age of sixty-nine. She wrote to a friend that this climb would be one of her last, "for it is wise at my age to drop the alpenstock before the alpenstock drops me."[7] She died six years later, in 1871—the same year that Lucy Walker would become the first woman to climb the Matterhorn.

By the middle of the nineteenth century, an increasing number of women—not Frenchwomen, it seems, but most of them British tourists—were beginning to venture off the increasingly popular paths of the Alps and to climb some of the nearby peaks. Perhaps the most ambitious of these early Alpine-travelers-cum-mountaineers was a woman known to us today only as Mrs. Henry Warwick Cole, whose climbs were modest but whose account of her journeys, published in 1859 as A Lady's Tour of Monte Rosa, was quite influential. Cole seems to have been the first to publicly encourage other women to take up mountaineering; after noting how men are "much disposed to magnify all its dangers, especially when they have to conduct a lady," she assured her readers that "any lady, blessed with moderate health and activity . . . may accomplish the Tour of Monte Rosa with great delight and few inconveniences."[8]

Cole was also the first Englishwoman to discuss the problem of dressing appropriately for climbing without wholly contravening the restrictive codes of the Victorian age. "A lady's dress is inconvenient for mountaineering," she wrote, "even under the most careful management, and therefore every device which may render it less so should be adopted." She advised women climbers to wear a broadbrimmed hat instead of carrying a parasol, to wear wool rather than cotton, and to give up fashionable footwear in favor of sturdy boots. She also suggested that rings be sewn into the seams of the dress "and a cord passed through them, the ends of which should be knotted together in such a way that the whole dress may be drawn up at a moment's notice to the requisite height." Otherwise, if the hemline is too low, "it catches the stones, especially when coming down hill, and sends them rolling on those below. I have heard more than one gentleman complain of painful blows suffered from such accidents."[9] (The pretexts will change, but "gentlemen" will continue to complain about the presence of women in a climbing party.)

The first Englishwoman to climb the highest and most challenging Alpine peaks on a regular basis was Lucy Walker. Introduced to climbing in 1859 by her father, she made nearly a hundred ascents over the following two decades, including an 1871 climb of the 14,782-foot Matterhorn. This ascent, the first by a woman of the most famous and most feared peak in the Alps, alerted the general public to the existence of women who climbed at a standard comparable to that of men. Many proper Victorians disapproved of Walker's feat, but the following verses, first published in Punch, indicate that others were at least nominally sympathetic:

No glacier can baffle, no precipice balk her,
No peak rise above her, however sublime.
Give three times three cheers for intrepid Miss Walker.
I say, my boys, doesn't she know how to climb![10]

This bit of doggerel, though not meant to be taken seriously, is nonetheless typical of contemporary reportage in that it was written by men for an implied audience of men; it acknowledged a woman's climbing accomplishment while simultaneously using phrases such as "my boys" to remind readers that the activity was still largely and properly male. Despite Cole's book of 1859, there was as yet no countervailing tradition of women writing for other women about their own climbs—a situation Walker did little to remedy, as she never wrote extensively about her own career. Her notoriety, however, helped to create a reading public for other, more literary-minded women alpinists, and soon a host of climbers and travelers—among them Amelia Edwards, Meta Brevoort, Nina Mazuchelli, Mrs. E. P. Jackson and Mary Mummery—were not only climbing but writing about it as well. Perhaps the most prolific of these climbing and writing women was Elizabeth Le Blond, who made dozens of daring climbs in both the Alps and the mountains of Norway and chronicled her adventures in some eight books.[11]

In America, for women and men alike, mountaineering caught on more slowly than in Europe, and until the end of the nineteenth century, there are few written accounts of American climbs by women. Julia Archibald Holmes, the daughter of a pioneering suffragist and herself a "bloomer girl"—an advocate of more sensible dress for women—made what appears to be the first woman's ascent of a high American summit by climbing Pikes Peak in 1858. Twenty-one years later, the famed British traveler Isabella Bird reached the top of Longs Peak, and, in 1890, Fay Fuller reached the top of Mount Rainier. Holmes's account of her Pikes Peak climb first appeared in *The Sibyl*, a journal published by women and devoted to a variety of social reforms, thus establishing from the very beginning a link between mountain climbing and feminism that would prove characteristic in America.[12]

None of these early American ascents could match those of the more accomplished British women, but if standards of technique and daring lagged behind in the United States, social acceptance of women's climbing seemed to be ahead. In the latter half of the nineteenth century, as Frances Cogan has pointed out, the prevailing American ideal of femininity—the "Cult of True Womanhood" which held that women should be delicate, submissive, and wan—was challenged by an alternative ideal that stressed robust health and strenuous physical activity for women.[13] This perhaps explains why the numerous mountain clubs which formed in North America around the turn of the century—foremost among them the Appalachian Mountain Club, the Sierra Club, and the Alpine Club of Canada—were open to both sexes from the beginning and actively encouraged women to climb. Featured in the official journals of these organizations were articles written by experienced outdoorswomen who not only offered the usual advice on clothing and camp life,[14] but also stressed the health benefits of outdoor recreation, a theme that was gradually elaborated until, by the early twentieth century, mountaineering was felt to provide relief not only from physical debility but also for a whole range of "nervous conditions" to which women were deemed susceptible. The benefits were more subtle and profound than mere fresh air and exercise. When a woman is climbing, wrote Mary Crawford in 1909,

> the whole attention is so absolutely concentrated on the business at hand that every worry is put to flight and nothing is of any moment beyond reaching the top of the mountain. The therapeutic value of this one feature alone is inestimable.
>
> Take the woman whose usual occupation is a sedentary one—whose daily life is one of routine in the office, the school-room, the sick-room; and who is constantly giving out to others her nervous energy. Put her on the train and send her to the mountains. . . . She is going to know herself as never before—physically, mentally, emotionally. And so she starts out, gains confidence with every step, finds the dangers she has imagined far greater than those she encounters and arrives at last upon the summit to gaze out upon a new world. Surely not the same earth she has seen all her life? Yes—but looked at from *on top*—a point of view which now makes upon her mind its indelible impression.[15]

The view from the mountaintop embraces more than mere scenery. Seemingly far removed from the strictures of society—at liberty, in the comparative utopia of the mountain wilderness, to use their bodies toward ends of their own—women climbers apply their previously divided energies to personal fulfillment rather than the care of others. And, in a metaphor charged with political meanings, every step upward offers a tantalizing vision of a "new world" of hitherto inaccessible possibilities.

Given the unmistakably feminist undercurrent of such rhetoric, it is hardly surprising that the first openly feminist mountaineers of genuine renown were Americans. Annie Smith Peck, an American who gained a measure of fame by climbing the Matterhorn in 1895, organized a series of expeditions to the Andes of South America and, in 1908, finally succeeded, with the financial backing of *Harper's Monthly Magazine*, in climbing Huascarán Norte, a 21,831-foot peak in Peru. Her motives were unabashedly feminist. She wished, as she later wrote, "to attain some height where no *man* had previously stood. . . . being always from earliest years a firm believer in the equality of the sexes, I felt that any great achievement in any line of endeavor would be of advantage to my sex."[16] Another American, Fanny Bullock Workman, compiled an even more impressive climbing record than Peck, exploring thousands of square miles of the Himalaya and climbing to nearly twenty-three thousand feet. For a time, she and Peck competed openly for the women's altitude record, a competition that was followed in newspapers and scientific journals and which Workman ultimately won. Like Peck, she was not satisfied merely to be able to climb on an equal basis with men. Workman demanded equality not just in the mountains, but also in the quotidian realm of lowland society, and she used her fame as a climber to further the cause of women's rights, once going so far as to have herself photographed high amid the Himalayan snows, displaying a banner that read "Votes for Women."[17]

The British women of this era, in contrast to their American sisters, climbed with little institutional support and in the face of considerably greater societal opposition. The Alpine Club, then as now Britain's premier mountaineering association, had been founded in 1857, but its feminine counterpart would not appear until 1907—when, largely through the efforts of Elizabeth Le Blond, the Ladies' Alpine Club finally came into being. In a society whose resources were so completely controlled by men, of course, there could be no real equality between the two organizations, and what many thought the only fair solution, the opening of the Alpine Club to both sexes, did not take place until 1976. In the meantime, the reactions of Alpine Club members to female accomplishments typically ranged from cool acceptance to outright hostility. Ellen Pigeon, who with her sister Anna had in 1869 made the first traverse of the Sesia Joch—a difficult glacier crossing on which Pigeon had to take over the leadership after their male guide lost first the way and then his nerve—wrote that many Alpine Club members refused to speak to her afterward.[18] Workman spoke openly about the unfriendly reception she occasionally received when lecturing in Britain; following her death in 1925, her obituary in the *Alpine Journal* would only admit, with revealing understatement, that Workman "felt that she suffered from 'sex antagonism,' and it is possible that some unconscious feeling, let us say of the novelty of a woman's intrusion into the domain of exploration so long reserved to man, may in some quarters have existed. . . . in time there tended to arise in certain high and serene circles an atmosphere, shall we say, of aloofness?"[19]

Such resistance was not confined to the Alpine Club; Elizabeth Le Blond encountered opposition even from her own family. "Stop her climbing mountains," her aunt once wrote to her mother. "She is scandalizing all London and looks like a Red Indian." Le Blond continued to climb in spite of such criticism, but like other British women climbers of the period, she seemed not to consider her mountaineering as part of a larger effort to improve the general status of women. In fact, many of the most accomplished British women, including the great Lucy Walker, remained quite conservative in all matters not touching on their right to climb mountains.[20]

By the turn of the century, British men were more willing to acknowledge the existence of women climbers, but only on the most condescending terms. In 1914, a popular and influential guidebook, Claude Benson's British Mountaineering, was revised to include a chapter on "Mountaineering for Ladies" in which the author suggested rather archly that "ladies should make *a special study of the art of tieing knots.* . . . I have heard it rumoured—that some lady mountaineers of repute are moderately helpless in these respects." His advice concerning clothing—that a proper-looking skirt, to be removed once out of sight of the nearest village, be worn over more practical and durable trousers—proved workable in practice, but it was clearly predicated upon the idea that there would inevitably be a man in the climbing party, a man who—as Mrs. Cole had hinted earlier—would inevitably perceive the presence of a woman as a burden: "the skirt . . . must be as light as possible, if only out of consideration for the man with the rucksack, for into that it *must* go at the foot of the climb."[21]

Much of "Mountaineering for Ladies" was, in fact, not addressed to women at all but to the men it was assumed would be in charge of them. Foremost among the dangers against which women must be guarded, Benson felt, was that of overtaxing themselves. Noting the contemporary medical opinion that "a woman who has *once* overwalked herself seems to be more or less an invalid for life" and that doctors, "in this age of feminine athletics, are constantly having girls on their hands who have overdone it, and will never be quite the same again," Benson advised men to "leave the ladies to set the pace, and never hurry them. On the contrary, keep on them a watchful eye. A general symptom of fatigue is not lifting the foot high enough, and so stumbling very slightly. If such a stumble be followed by an increase of pace and an unconvincing laugh, you may be *quite sure*, and the rate of going must be *unostentatiously* slackened. Unostentatiously, because under such circumstances, ladies detest being made a fuss over."[22]

The problem with such patronizing attitudes—so clearly grounded in a male belief in female inferiority—was not merely that they were insulting, but that they worked to prevent women from being anything *but* second-rate climbers. Mountaineers do not develop sound judgment by being watched over—and certainly not by being made to feel guilty over slowing the pace and "burdening" the men in the party—but only by being watchful themselves, by observing and responding appropriately to the exigencies of an ascent. To become fully competent, women would have to do more than merely travel up and down the peaks; they would also have to find the safest route, interpret signs of threatening weather and assume the comparatively greater risk of climbing at the front of the rope. They would, in other words, have to *lead*. Not surprisingly, given the precedent set by such women as Holmes, Workman, and Peck, the first woman to express and exemplify this idea clearly was an American, Miriam O'Brien. As early as the 1920s, O'Brien "realized that the person who invariably climbs behind a good leader, guide or amateur, may never really learn mountaineering at all," because it is the leader who "solves the immediate problems of technique, tactics and strategy as they occur."[23] Without the experience of leading, climbers cannot realize their full potential, and it was for this reason that the best male alpinists had long before decided to climb without the assistance of native guides. In addition, O'Brien realized that women, in order to explore their own limits, would have to climb not only guideless but "manless" as well: If women "were really to lead, that is, to take the entire responsibility for the climb, there couldn't be any man at all in the party," since "in any emergency . . . what man wouldn't spring to the front and take over?"[24] In the summer of 1929, she put her theory into practice by making a series of sensational, manless ascents in the Chamonix area, first the Aiguille du Peigne, which she climbed with Winifred Marples, and then, with Alice Damesme in the lead, the Grépon—at the time still one of the most difficult and respected of climbs, more famous among rockclimbing specialists than even the Matterhorn.

These and other climbs done *en cordée féminine*—that is, as a women's ro[.]-team—were big news in the climbing world. Some of the response to these feats was quite positive, perhaps even *too* positive. After the first manless ascent of the Matterhorn, for example, the rather conservative Groupe de Haute Montagne threw the successful climbers an elaborate party, complete with flowers, speeches, and a band. And the man who had been led up the Grépon immediately ahead of O'Brien and Damesme, and who felt himself humiliated for having made use of a professional guide on a day that women had proved themselves able to dispense with one, nonetheless had the grace to applaud the two women as they reached the summit. Others were more hostile. "The Grépon has disappeared," lamented one man. "Of course there are still some rocks standing there, but as a climb it no longer exists. Now that it has been done by two women alone no self-respecting man can undertake it. A pity, too, because it used to be a very good climb." Even the *New York Times* denigrated the accomplishment, reporting it under the headline "An Easy Day for a Lady," a reference to A. F. Mummery's famous remark that "all mountains appear doomed to pass through three stages: An inaccessible peak—The most difficult ascent in the Alps—An easy day for a lady."[25]

In the 1930s, partly in response to O'Brien's sensational climbs and partly, no doubt, in response to the continuing growth of women's climbing organizations, such as the Ladies' Alpine Club and the Pinnacle Club (founded in 1921), the *cordée féminine* became an increasingly common sight in the Alps and on the rock climbs of the British Isles.[26] More and more women carried out their own climbs, improving their skills dramatically and creating an international network of highly competent climbers. Following the hiatus of the Second World War, these mountaineers began organizing expeditions of their own, not only to the Alps, but also to the highest ranges of the world. In 1950, Claude Kogan and Nicole Leininger made a *cordée féminine* ascent of 19,816-foot Qitaraju, in the Peruvian Andes—at the time the highest altitude reached by women on their own. Five years later the first all-women's Himalayan expedition succeeded in climbing 22,000-foot Gyalgen Peak in Nepal. Several other women's expeditions followed, including Kogan's attempt on the giant Cho Oyu in 1959, the 1961 British Women's Kulu Expedition, and the 1965 Indian Women's Expedition to Mrigthuni. Most ambitious of all was the 1975 Japanese Women's Expedition to Mount Everest, whose leader, Junko Tabei, in the year declared by the United Nations as International

Women's Year, became the first woman to climb to the highest point on earth.[27] Since then, women have continued to explore the limits of what was previously thought possible not only for women, but for all climbers. The Polish mountaineer Wanda Rutkiewicz, for example, after climbing Mount Everest in 1978, went on in 1985 to ascend 26,657-foot Nanga Parbat with an all-women expedition that did not, as is traditionally done, make use of supplemental oxygen supplies. She has since climbed two more of the world's highest summits, 26,286-foot Xixabangma, and 28,250-foot K2, the second highest peak in the world and a much more difficult climb than Everest. Only a very few men can match Rutkiewicz's record—evidence of the recent narrowing of the "gender gap" between male and female mountaineers. Among rockclimbing specialists, in fact, that gap may have already closed: by 1987, writers in the climbing press were openly speculating that Lynn Hill was not merely the greatest contemporary woman rock climber, but "maybe the best climber, period."[28]

In summing up the history of women's mountaineering in her book *Women on the Rope*, Cicely Williams insisted—rather disingenuously—that sexism had rarely been a limiting factor for women climbers. As early as 1910, she claimed, the position of women generally and women climbers in particular had been "recognised and applauded on all sides; no longer need they struggle for their freedom; that contest had been fought and won." By the time her book was published in 1973, Williams felt confident enough to claim that women climbers had "won for themselves the respect of even the most anti-feminine members" of the prestigious (but still, significantly enough, all-male) Alpine Club. The situation in the 1970s, she believed, was "a happy one," with any remaining disparities between men's and women's accomplishments being attributable not to culture but to nature, to the seemingly inarguable fact that "men are, on the whole, better climbers than women and . . . have greater reserves of strength."[29] Even as *Women on the Rope* went to press, however, there was evidence that the situation was not so happy after all. There were, for example, apocryphal stories, such as the one about the two women, with ropes and other climbing gear slung over their shoulders, hiking up toward the base of a peak. Along the way they pass a man who asks, "Are you alone?"—as if, in spite of the long history of the *cordée féminine*, two women attempting an ascent without a man were somehow "alone." Then there is "Bob," the imaginary character invented by women climbers tired of hearing unsolicited advice from male passersby: "When men come up as the women work out the problems of their route, they discuss Bob's advice about the moves. Appearing to be reassured that the women are adequately supervised by Bob, the men do not linger as long as they might, but move on to their own climb."[30]

In these examples we hardly sense the "respect" insisted upon by Williams, but rather the familiar sexism that stems both from male doubts about women's ability and male anxiety about women usurping the role of "leader." The problem goes deeper than this, however. In 1969, for example, Arlene Blum—a feminist and climber who dismissed Williams's book as a "ladylike history"—was refused a place on an expedition to climb a 21,090-foot peak in Afghanistan, in spite of her qualifications. The expedition leader acknowledged her experience and proven ability to perform at high altitudes, but insisted that "one woman and nine men would seem to me to be unpleasant high on the open ice, not only in excretory situations, but in the easy masculine companionship which is so vital a part of the joy of an expedition." Underlying this argument is the idea that climbing is not so much about the application of skill in overcoming a challenge as it is about male bonding. According to this line of reasoning, a woman climber's qualifications are irrelevant; climbing is almost by definition a *masculine* activity whose essential joy (for men) would evaporate in the presence of the feminine. It is in this context—the equation of climbing and masculinity—that we must interpret the comment by a male climber that "there are no good women climbers," because they "either aren't good climbers, or they aren't real women."[31] A good climber, after all, is commonly thought to be bold, skillful, self-reliant, courageous, and strong—all that men are "supposed" to be, and all that women are "supposed" not to be. When women climb well, and when they do so unaccompanied by men, they challenge not just individual male egos but the whole constellation of assumptions about gender in our society.

Little is really surprising in all of this; similar sexism has been encountered by women attempting to enter many other traditionally male fields. The more interesting question, I think, is not why men want women *out* of climbing, but why women want *in*—a question raised in 1978 when Arlene Blum sought the imprimatur of the American Alpine Club for a women's expedition to the dangerous, 26,504-

foot peak known as Annapurna. (The club's approval was necessary because without it the government of Nepal would not issue the expedition a climbing permit.) One club member, Grant Barnes, citing the very real hazards of Himalayan climbing, argued that women should stay off the highest peaks not because women are underqualified, but because, in some vague moral sense, they are *over*qualified. "One can understand," he wrote, "the macho heroics of young and sometimes not-so-young men who continue to push their personal limits till they are dead or disabled—their absurdity is socially and perhaps hormonally programmed." But women are supposed to be too sensible and mature, possessed of too genuine a sense of values, for such foolishness, and therefore "should not sacrifice life on the same altar of egoism that causes men to join the Marines, shoot buffalo, fight over women."[32]

Here again is an argument for excluding women from climbing which is based on the idea that the sport is essentially masculine, although this time it is identified with what Barnes considered the worst, rather than the best, of traditional masculinity. As an excuse not to approve a permit, of course, such reasoning could hardly be taken seriously—for one thing, it rather too conveniently ignores the positive attributes of climbing that had been identified decades before by women like Mary Crawford—and indeed it was rejected by the American Alpine Club, which in due time gave its approval to Blum's expedition.

Barnes's argument does, however, raise a larger issue, that of the values which are embodied in sport and physical activity in general—an issue which has also engaged the interest of feminist scholars. Lois Bryson, for example, has questioned the traditional "liberal" wisdom of striving merely to provide equal access to sport without also challenging sport's anti-feminist underpinnings. "Involvement in sport raises for women similar issues to those raised by involvement in the world of business and employment," she wrote. "Are we to take up places in the current system on men's terms, when it is clear that it has been created by men and they control it? Since women have different interests would these not be better served by a changed or a separate system rather than squeezing into the existing one?" Similarly, Roberta Bennett and others have written that, in their current forms, "sport, play, and games . . . perpetuate male dominance and female oppression." Acknowledging the difficulty of changing current attitudes, Bryson concluded that sport may be "so thoroughly masculinized that it seems unlikely that it can be reclaimed to serve women's interests."[33]

What would a sport that reflects "women's interests" look like? Bennett wrote that "one can envision changing the means by which successes are defined and measured, so that the value would be in cooperative growth and in seeking mutual joy in one another's accomplishments rather than in the annihilation of an opponent. One can envision shared decision-making, shared knowledge, a return of control of sport to the performers, and their empowerment as subjects rather than their oppression as objects." At the very least, she added, feminist sport would lack such features of traditional sport as competition, the "destruction" of one's opponent, the buying, selling, and trading of athletes, and a relationship between coaches and players that ranges between paternalism and dictatorship.[34] Most mountaineers, I think, will immediately recognize in this description a number of features that have *always* been absent from climbing—features whose absence not only distinguishes mountaineering from traditional sport but also makes it eminently "reclaimable," to borrow Bryson's term, to serve feminist interests. Climbing does not, for example, depend for its drama on the vanquishing of an adversary; though climbers occasionally speak figuratively of the mountain itself as an "opponent," it is really neither sensible nor necessary to do so, and many prefer to picture the mountain as a neutral entity, as the field on which their game is played or the stage on which their drama is enacted. Similarly, the shared joy of climbing, the exchange of support and encouragement as first one climber and then another venture ahead to make the route, has long been recognized as an integral part of the mountaineering experience.

What most clearly sets climbing apart from other sports, however, is a feature often seen as a weakness but which is really, I think, a strength: climbing's lack of, or perhaps more properly its resistance to, any kind of centralized organization. Traditional sport is built upon a complex set of hierarchies—players and captains, coaches and owners, umpires and commissioners—at whose apex stands a supreme authority, typically male, who wields power for "the good of the game." These structures promulgate and enforce both the rules and the meanings of the game, not democratically but paternalistically, according to criteria that have little to do with the players' own desires but everything to do with the game's continued social propriety (and, ultimately, its commercial viability). To see this it is only necessary to consider the debates that have attended such rule changes as those allowing the three-point shot in professional basketball (designed to keep the game commercially attractive), allowing girls to play in various youth sports programs (a debate pitting social equality against social propriety), and prohibiting the use of steroids (a complex issue involving social, commercial, and other concerns).

Mountaineering, by contrast, has generally been both commercially and socially marginal, which may be why it has produced nothing even remotely resembling the extensive, centralized superstructures of conventional sport—nothing comparable to the National Basketball Association, the National Collegiate Athletic Association, or even the Little League.[35] In climbing, the rules are not handed down as some sort of unquestionable fiat from on high; in fact, there are really no "rules" at all, for without any authoritarian structure, without any *enforcer* of the rules, the concept itself does not quite make sense. Climbers themselves speak not of *rules* but of *style:* to climb a difficult cliff or peak in a direct and simple manner, without undue reliance on technological assistance, is to climb in "good style," to merit the admiration of one's peers, and perhaps most important, to become totally absorbed in the climb itself and afterward feel a genuine sense of accomplishment. The notion of what constitutes good style is constantly in flux and evolves out of an ongoing process of discussion and negotiation. Such discussion occasionally takes place under the auspices of official organizations, such as the American Alpine Club, but the action of such bodies—which in any event is never binding on individual climbers—is generally no more than to ratify the temporary consensus reached earlier, typically in myriad informal discussions over mountain campfires and the seemingly endless exchanges of letters-to-the-editor in the climbing press.[36]

Debates over style, as noted above, are primarily (though not exclusively) concerned with the types of technological aid that may be used without compromising the climber's sense of achievement. As Lito Tejada-Flores wrote in an influential essay entitled, appropriately enough, "The Games Climbers Play," a good style "preserve(s) the climber's feeling of personal . . . accomplishment against the *meaninglessness* of a success which *represents* merely technological victory"[37]—a characterization that makes explicit what is often only implicit in traditional sport: the connection between rules and *meanings,* the fact that sport represents certain values. The rigid hierarchies of traditional sport operate to control those meanings, to ensure that the game does not undermine the received values of the sponsoring society. The meanings expressed in mountaineering, by contrast, are determined communally by climbers themselves; reflecting the values of a comparatively small group—a group, moreover, with a tradition of independence, even eccentricity—those meanings may at least potentially challenge, rather than support, the values of society.[38] Just as important as the rules themselves, it should be added, is the process through which climbers adopt them. Communal, constantly in flux, and based on consensus rather than a hierarchical concentration of power, that process resembles the idealized politics of a feminist utopia more than the male model exemplified by traditional sport.

It should hardly be surprising, then, that women have been able to "reclaim" climbing for feminist ends more successfully than they have other sports. I have already noted how mountaineers such as Annie Peck and Fannie Bullock Workman appropriated climbing to serve their feminist politics; a more recent example is Arlene Blum's 1978 American Women's Himalayan Expedition, which not only succeeded in climbing Annapurna—the tenth highest mountain in the world and widely recognized as a difficult objective—but also, I think, quite successfully embodied a feminist worldview.

Though they are all part of the same women's mountaineering tradition, it is important at this point to note the differences between Blum's Annapurna expedition and the climbs that preceded it. For all their value as feminist propagandists and role models, both Peck and Workman climbed in ways that ultimately reflected, and even reinforced, the values of the patriarchal society they sought to change. Peck, for example, habitually wrote about her achievements using the most sexist of metaphors, as if the apogee of a woman's existence could be to "conquer" a "virgin" summit.[39] And both climbers organized their expeditions into hierarchies that replicated many of the injustices of nineteenth-century imperial society: at the top was a wealthy, all-powerful, Caucasian leader (albeit in these cases a woman leader); just below, typically, was a sort of middle class, the Swiss guides who signed on primarily to earn a good salary; and at the very bottom were the native porters, who were paid only a pittance and were generally considered more or less expendable. (Workman in particular was known to be callous toward native peoples.)[40]

It was not until later that these values, typical of what might be called the traditional male expedition model, began to be widely questioned; the Annapurna expedition seems to have been the first to conspicuously repudiate the patriarchal model in favor of the sort of egalitarian communalism that had always been latent in the climbing experience. In *Annapurna: A Woman's Place*, Blum's account of the expedition, the difference is apparent at once. The book has a more open and inclusive feel than its typical male counterpart; missing are the traditional photos of the leader forging heroically upward, and in their place we find group photos of team members working, talking and playing together. Where the traditional expedition narrative often effaces the role of indigenous people in an expedition, Blum's book includes numerous photos of the native Sherpas, whose portraits are reproduced in the same size and displayed just as prominently as those of the western members of the expedition. The text likewise reflects the natives' concerns as they work their way up the mountain with women who are clearly not merely their employers, but also their teammates.

These differences between *Annapurna* and the typical male expedition book reflect similar differences embodied in the ascent itself. It might seem odd to suggest that feminist mountaineers actually *climb* differently from men—after all, steep terrain and the techniques needed to negotiate it would seem to be the same for all—but there is more to climbing than just glaciers and cliffs. Some of the greatest challenges are personal, involving questions of motivation and psychological endurance, and others, particularly on the giant peaks of the Himalaya, are interpersonal tests of a group's ability to work together toward a common goal. One of the most telling aspects of the Annapurna expedition is the way the women handled the arguments and factions that seem inevitably to be a part of Himalayan climbing. Brought on in part by the strain of working for long periods under harsh conditions, such divisions can be crippling. "The questions of who will lead and who will make up the summit teams," Blum wrote, "invariably cause problems on large expeditions. Frequently the climbers divide into competing factions, and sometimes the losing faction has actually given up and gone home. More than one expedition has been seriously weakened by the bitterness resulting from these difficult choices." In fact, the leader of an expedition which had preceded Blum's group on Annapurna told her that had his teammates not reached the summit when they did, "the accumulated psychological strain would have forced them to abandon the attempt."[41]

Blum was well aware that one of the recurring doubts about women's expeditions had been whether women could work together as well as men;[42] recognizing how poorly previous expeditions had often met this particular challenge, the Annapurna team met with a clinical psychologist to study group dynamics before leaving for Nepal—a form of preparation which might have been scoffed at by men but which appears to have come in very handy on Annapurna. When, for example, the other climbers objected to one team member's constant complaining, Blum's response was a sterling example of effective communication, conveying the necessary sentiment without alienating the listener: "You know, Margi, you do as much work as anybody else and help me a lot with planning, but you complain so much that you don't get credit for all your hard work." The team's interpersonal skills were put to their severest test during a crucial meeting called to discuss the issue that had so often proved explosive on men's expeditions: who would do the lead climbing and who would climb in the less prestigious support roles. More precisely, the topic at issue was *how* such decisions would be made, and the consensus that was ultimately reached, after a lengthy and often tense discussion, was in the end less important than the openness and egalitarianism that had made the meeting possible in the first place. The process was itself the product, and when the meeting was over, Blum noted that the team was considerably strengthened by the fact that the climbers "had not simply buried [their] hurt feelings and gone marching stoically up the mountain."[43]

Blum's handling of such issues stands in sharp contrast to the more hierarchical approach favored within the masculine model. When Lopsang Tsering, the Nepalese official in charge of the expedition's Sherpa assistants, began losing control of his charges, Blum speculated that the problem might be his training as an Indian military officer. "The authoritarian way he dealt with subordinates might have worked well in the Army," she wrote, "but it antagonized the Sherpas, who seemed to no longer like or respect him. Lopsang in turn had reacted to his loss of control over the Sherpas with high blood pressure, incipient ulcers, and insomnia. He told Liz and me that he was through with climbing."[44] Lopsang's loss was really twofold: he was not only unable to do his job, but was also unable to savor what might have been an enjoyable experience.

If we agree with Blum that her team's ability to work together was a crucial factor in their eventual success, then her skillful interpersonal management emerges as itself a sort of "climbing technique," one just as valuable as the ability to climb steep rock and ice and a technique at which her team proved exceptionally adept. It might not be coincidental that, before Blum's expedition succeeded on Annapurna, nine out of thirteen men's attempts had failed. To the early claims that women could not climb as "well" as men, the women's success offers a marvelous rebuttal—one which not only proves the critics wrong but also prompts a thorough reexamination of what it means to climb, critiquing both a patriarchal climbing style and the social conventions that support it, offering in their place a perfectly viable feminist alternative.

In the past hundred and fifty years, women mountaineers have written more than a hundred books and several hundred more magazine articles about their adventures, and to narrow the field down to the sixteen selections included here was not easy. In doing so I was guided by several criteria. I wanted, first of all, to include enough early accounts to do justice to the long tradition of women in climbing. I did not, however, include only those accomplishments that were at the cutting edge of the sport—because the most thrilling ascents have not always resulted in the most compellingly written stories, and because I wanted this anthology to be a record of literary as well as climbing achievement. Besides, one can argue that the really significant history, in climbing as in any other field, is that made by more ordinary people, the mass of modest talents whose experiences also deserve to be recounted (though I cannot think of any of the climbers whose work is included here as being quite ordinary).

In choosing which portions of longer works to include, I was likewise guided by a number of concerns. I did not automatically choose to excerpt the climactic chapter in which the climbers triumphantly reach their summit. Such chapters may (or may not) be the most exciting part of a given account (nor do climbers always reach their summits), but they have a sameness about them that reflects one of the curious facts about mountains—namely, that the higher one climbs on them the more they begin to look alike. The lifeless zone of ice and snow about the summit is where mountains differ least; it is on their lower slopes, where the climber encounters the full diversity of alpine ecosystems and must interact with people of genuinely different cultures, that the greatest variety of experience is found. Besides, for many women climbers, the greatest challenge has come in the very earliest stages of the expedition, when they must overcome the doubt and disapproval of a society that would prefer they simply stay at home. I wanted this anthology to reflect something of the full variety of the climbing game, not just the attainment of a summit.

I also hope that these accounts will highlight what I feel is one of the most important, but underemphasized, aspects of the sport. Of the many meanings that have been read into climbing—it has at various times been seen as a metaphor for imperialistic conquest, spiritual ascent, arrogant self-aggrandizement, ascetic self-negation, or simple death wish—there is one, rather more mundane and personal, that has not received enough attention, and that is the view of climbing as an expression of caring and responsibility. For all except the solo climber, mountaineering is of necessity a highly interpersonal affair. Arlene Blum, for instance, insisted that she first fell in love with the sport simply because "the mountains were the best place to *know people* and to be happy,"[45] and for the great majority of less dedicated climbers the enjoyment of simple friendship in a beautiful environment is perhaps the most frequently cited reason for climbing. The sport's most basic rhythm, it seems to me, is that of one climber advancing cautiously while the other tends the rope in order to safeguard her—an ethic of reciprocal caring and support that is always latent in the climbing experience but tends to be repressed in the mountaineering narrative, which traditionally attempts to embody in its place an outmoded ethic of personal glory, domination, and conquest.

This alternation of risk and responsibility—for climbers perhaps the most compelling reality of their sport and for readers, I hope, a compelling symbol—is captured wonderfully in the term *cordée féminine*, the women's rope-team, two friends linked together in a dialectic of mutual ambition and mutual support. It symbolizes the sort of "shared joy" which feminists hope can transform sport in general, the joy that must have been felt by the Annapurna climbers as they watched two of their teammates, Irene Miller and Vera Komarkova, after weeks of hard and dangerous work, make the final climb to the summit. "They're doing it!" said one of the climbers. "I just know they're going to make it. It's so beautiful to watch. Deep blue sky, a plume of snow blowing off the top, and our friends way up there."

NOTES

The epigraphs are from Emily Kelly, "The Pinnacle Club," p. 324; and Elizabeth Le Blond, *Day In, Day Out*, p. 90.

1. There are scattered references to other early ascents as well. A minor peak called the Montanvert was climbed by a Madame Harsberg in 1788; in

1799, a Miss Parminter reportedly climbed "on," but apparently not to the top of, Le Buet in the Alps of Savoy, and other women appear to have ascended Le Buet in 1806. In 1822, two Scotswomen, a mother-daughter team known to us today only as Mrs. and Miss Campbell, crossed the snow-covered Col du Géant, a formidable pass on the Alpine frontier between France and Italy. Anne Lister ascended her first mountain in the Pyrenees in 1830, a woman identified only as a "Bavarian Princess" is said to have climbed the 10,328-foot Mittaghorn in 1834, and four years later Henriette d'Angeville became the second woman to reach the top of Mont Blanc (and, it is generally agreed, the first woman actually to *climb* it, as Paradis was reportedly carried much of the way to the summit). See Francis Henry Gribble, *The Early Mountaineers,* p. 240; Carroll Seghers, *The Peak Experience: Hiking and Climbing for Women,* p. 2; and Mary E. Crawford, "Mountain Climbing for Women," p. 85. The best treatments of the early history of women in mountaineering are Cicely Williams, *Women on the Rope: The Feminine Share in Mountain Adventure* and Bill Birkett and Bill Peascod, *Women Climbing: 200 Years of Achievement.* The subject is discussed at much less length in Gribble as well as in Arlene Blum, *Annapurna: A Woman's Place;* Ronald William Clark, *The Victorian Mountaineers;* Claire Éliane Engel, *Mountaineering in the Alps;* and James Ramsey Ullman, *The Age of Mountaineering.* Shirley Angell's *Pinnacle Club: A History of Women Climbing* is a useful in-house history of the first women's rockclimbing club, founded in Britain in 1921.

2. Williams, pp. 27–31. Lister's diaries have been edited by Helena Whitbread and published as *I Know My Own Heart: The Diaries of Anne Lister. 1791–1840* (London: Virago, 1988), but this collection does not include the brief entries concerning Lister's mountaineering in the Pyrenees.

3. Henriette d'Angeville, *Mon Excursion au Mont-Blanc en 1838,* pp. 29–30. A good English-language discussion of d'Angeville's climb is found in Williams, pp. 20–27. Earlier accounts of the climb—some of which contradict both Williams and d'Angeville on many particulars—include "Ascent of Mont-Blanc by a Lady," *The Annual Register, or a Review of the History and Politics of the Year 1838* (London: J. G. & F. Rivington, 1839), pp. 136–37; Stéphen d'Arve [Edmund de Catelin], *Histoire du Mont Blanc et de la Vallée de Chamonix,* pp. 83–85; J. S. Buckingham, *Belgium, the Rhine, Switzerland, and Holland. An Autumnal Tour,* Vol. II, pp. 190–92; J. Corcelle, *Mlle. Henriette d'Angeville. Une Ascension célèbre au Mont-Blanc* (1838); Émile Gaillard, *Une ascension romantique en 1838: Henriette d'Angeville au Mont-Blanc;* Charles Gos, *Pres de Névés et des Glaciers: Impressions Alpestres.* 5th ed., pp. 221–28; Chr[istian]. Müller, "Ascent of Mont Blanc, by Mademoiselle d'Angeville," pp. 387–91; and (perhaps the most reliable of the lot) Mary Paillon, "Mademoiselle d'Angeville: Notice Biographique," in *Annuaire du Club Alpin Français.*

4. D'Angeville, "A Letter to Markham Sherwill," in *Mont Blanc: An Anthology,* ed. Claire Éliane Engel, p. 110.

5. D'Angeville, *Mon Excursion*, pp. 21, 25.

6. Claire Éliane Engel, *A History of Mountaineering in the Alps*, pp. 67–68.

7. Quoted in Gribble, *The Early Mountaineers*, p. 249.

8. Mrs. Henry Warwick Cole, *A Lady's Tour Round Monte Rosa; with Visits to the Italian Valleys . . . in the Years 1850–56–58*, pp. 12, 391–92.

9. Ibid., pp. 6–8.

10. "In Memoriam: Miss Lucy Walker." *Alpine Journal* 31 (February 1917), p. 98.

11. See Amelia Ann Blanford Edwards, *Untrodden Peaks and Unfrequented Valleys: A Midsummer Ramble in the Dolomites* and Nina E. Mazuchelli, *The Indian Alps and How We Crossed Them*. Typical of Elizabeth Le Blond's books is *High Life and Towers of Silence*. The work of Brevoort, Jackson, and Mummery may be sampled in this anthology. The idea that women were climbing the most difficult peaks in the Alps apparently became such a commonplace that it could be parodied, as it was, for example, in an H. G. Wells story in which the protagonist's elderly mother climbs a difficult peak, descends by means of a tremendous avalanche, and remains nonplussed through it all. See H. G. Wells, "Little Mother Up the Mörderberg," *Golden Book Magazine* 9 (April 1929), pp. 53–57, and reprinted in *H. G. Wells Short Stories*, ed. Tim Heald (London: Folio Society, 1990), pp. 201–10. For a discussion of the early fictional treatment of women mountain climbers, see Claire Éliane Engel, "Early Lady Climbers," pp. 51–59.

12. See Julia Archibald Holmes, *A Bloomer Girl on Pike's Peak, 1858*; Isabella Bird, *A Lady's Life in the Rocky Mountains*; and Fay Fuller, "A Trip to the Summit."

13. Frances B. Cogan, *All-American Girl: The Ideal of Real Womanhood in Mid-Nineteenth-Century America*, pp. 3–4.

14. See, for example, Miss M. F. Whitman, "Camp Life for Ladies," *Appalachia* 2 (1879–1881), pp. 44–48, and Mrs. L. D. Pychoska, "Walking Dress for Ladies," *Appalachia* 5 (1887–1889), pp. 28–30.

15. Crawford, pp. 87–88.

16. Annie Smith Peck, *A Search for the Apex of America: High Mountain Climbing in Peru and Bolivia*, p. x. Peck describes her Matterhorn ascent in *Up the Matterhorn . . .* and her Huascarán climb in both *High Mountain Climbing* and "The First Ascent of Mount Huascaran," *Harper's Monthly Magazine* 118 (January 1909), pp. 173–87.

17. Workman is discussed at length in Dorothy Middleton, *Victorian Lady Travellers*. Workman published numerous magazine articles and, in conjunction with her husband, William Hunter Workman, five books. Representative of her work are "Recent First Ascents in the Himalaya," and *Call of the Snowy Hispar: Narrative of Exploration and Mountaineering on the Northern Frontier of India*. The debate over the altitude record can be sampled in Workman, "Miss Peck and Mrs. Workman," p. 143, and Peck, "Miss Peck Replies to Mrs.

Workman," p. 183. The "Votes for Women" photograph is reproduced in Middleton, p. 83.
18. Williams, pp. 48–49; Clark, pp. 175–76.
19. Farrar, J. P. "In Memoriam: Mrs. Fanny Bullock Workman," p. 182.
20. Clark, pp. 176–78.
21. Claude Ernest Benson, *British Mountaineering*, pp. 184–85.
22. Ibid., pp. 186–88.
23. Miriam Underhill (O'Brien), *Give Me the Hills*, p. 149. As early as 1921, the founders of the Pinnacle Club wrote explicitly of the importance of leading: "In climbing with men where 'the best must lead,' women have little opportunity to master, or to enjoy, the finer points and sensations of the art itself" (qtd. in Angell, p. 15). But O'Brien seems to have been the first to apply this idea to the harder climbs of the day and to gain notoriety for doing so.
24. Ibid., p. 150.
25. Ibid., pp. 158, 169; *New York Times* (September 7, 1929); and Albert Frederick Mummery, *My Climbs in the Alps and Caucasus*, p. 160.
26. See Angell, pp. 51–58, for an indication of how many *cordées féminines* were active at this time.
27. See Nicole Leininger and Georges Kogan, *The Ascent of Alpamayo: An Account of the Franco-Belgian Expedition to the Cordillera Blanca in the High Andes*; Monica Jackson and Elizabeth Stark, *Tents in the Clouds: The First Women's Himalayan Expedition*; Josephine Scarr, *Four Miles High*; Joyce Dunsheath, "Mrigthuni, Garhwal," p. 472; and Junko Tabei, *Everest Mother*.
28. John Steiger, "Lynn Hill," p. 49; for Wanda Rutkiewicz, see Birkett and Peascod, pp. 131–47.
29. Williams, pp. 17, 106, 226–27.
30. Sallie Greenwood, "Frame of Reference: A Historical Perspective," p. 46.
31. Blum, pp. 1, 251.
32. Quoted in ibid., pp. 2–3.
33. Lois Bryson, "Sport and the Maintenance of Masculine Hegemony," *Women's Studies International Forum* 10 (1987), pp. 350, 358; and Roberta Bennett, K. Gail Whitaker, Nina Jo Woolley Smith, and Anne Sablove, "Changing the Rules of the Game: Reflections Toward a Feminist Analysis of Sport," *Women's Studies International Forum* 10 (1987), p. 370.
34. Bennett et al., p. 378.
35. There is an international climbing organization, the Union Internationale des Associations d'Alpinisme, or UIAA, but its primary role has been to promote safety standards for equipment (such as the breaking strength of ropes); it does not in any direct sense govern the way people choose to climb.
36. Some of the differences between traditional sport and decentralized sports, such as climbing, could possibly parallel differences between female and male psychological development in our culture. Carol Gilligan, for exam-

ple, in *In a Different Voice* (Cambridge: Harvard University Press, 1982), has noted that in games, children "learn respect for rules and come to understand the ways rules can be made and changed" (p. 9); citing the research of Janet Lever, she notes how boys become "increasingly fascinated with the legal elaboration of rules and the development of fair procedures for adjudicating conflicts," whereas girls "are more tolerant in their attitude toward rules, more willing to make exceptions, and more easily reconciled to innovations" (p. 10).

37. Lito Tejada-Flores, "The Games Climbers Play," p. 23, my emphasis.

38. If climbing affords a position from which one can challenge the received values of a society, it is probably no coincidence that so many pioneering environmentalists—John Muir, John Burroughs, Arne Naess, David Brower—were also climbers.

39. Peck, *A Search for the Apex of America*, p. x.

40. Middleton, p. 84.

41. Blum, pp. 108, 117.

42. "Annapurna Climb Called an Inspiration to Women," *New York Times* (October 14, 1978).

43. Blum, pp. 49, 56, 114–19.

44. Ibid., p. 172.

45. Ibid., p. 20, my emphasis.

«I saucily declined the proffered help»

Mrs. Cole Climbs the Aeggischhorn and
Attempts the Pic de Grivola, 1850 and 1858

Between 1850 and 1858, Mrs. Henry Warwick Cole made three
extended trips to the Alps, completely circling 15,203-foot
Monte Rosa and climbing several of the minor peaks rising on
its periphery. The account she wrote of her adventures, an
attractively produced volume titled *A Lady's Tour Round Monte
Rosa* and published in 1859, was apparently the first in English
by a woman alpinist. Unfortunately we know very little about
Cole today, not even her own name, which appears only as
"Mrs. Henry Warwick Cole" in her publications. (We know that
Henry was something of a legal expert, the author of a book on
the legal issues confronting English citizens living in France.)

Mrs. Cole's own writing indicates she was well read in several languages, with tastes that ran toward Shakespeare, Wordsworth, and Ruskin, but that also included works on travel and
geography. Much of her writing today seems conventional, rely-
ing perhaps too easily on contemporary clichés of the "sublime"
in mountain scenery, but at times it is original and elegant,
commenting perceptively on both the mountain landscape and
the native people who were her guides and hosts. Like many
travel writers, she was not above poking fun at what to her eth-
nocentric British readers must have seemed backward customs
and culinary habits. But, as she pointed out at the beginning of
her book, she had written expressly to encourage other women
to travel and climb in the Alps, and she thus also made sure to
note the many changes which were then making Alpine travel

more agreeable to cultured British visitors—the stove that no longer smoked, the Italian innkeeper who learned English, the solicitous guides who constructed a comfortable stone couch for her as she waited out a mountain storm.

In the excerpt below, reprinted from A Lady's Tour, Cole describes her 1850 climb of the minor peak known as the Aeggischhorn, and her more ambitious, if unsuccessful, attempt of 1858 on the 13,022-foot Pic de Grivola.

ON REACHING the Hôtel de la Jungfrau, the landlord warmly welcomed us, conducted us to the best rooms in his then half-built inn, and made us as comfortable as he could. He was an Italian, and was delighted to talk in his native language with our American companion. He could not then speak English, but has since visited our country and learned our language, as an additional means of making himself agreeable to English travellers. In the evening the stove in the *salle-à-manger* smoked, a fault which has since been remedied; and therefore, as it was too cold to sit without a fire at so great an elevation, we went down into the guides' room below, which was equally large, and there the genial warmth of a wood fire was really quite enjoyable, though, during the day, we had suffered so much from the heat. The landlord, guides, and porters played at cards at an adjoining table, and none seemed in the least degree disturbed by our presence, whilst we, equally at our ease, wrote letters; and then my companions in turn selected and read aloud some favourite sonnets from a pocket edition of Shakespere [sic]. The landlord assured us that if we intended to see the view on the following morning from the summit of the mountain, it would, at that season, be necessary to be there at daybreak, before the mists arose from the valley, which they always do shortly after the sun has risen.

Sept. 7.—We were awakened by our alarum at a quarter to 4 A.M., had a hasty breakfast, and left the hotel by 5.10 A.M. The gentlemen walked as usual, and I rode "Fritz." After ascending for above thirty-five minutes we had a fine view of the Strahlhorn and Weisshorn, and beyond them, in the far distance, which the rising sun had just reached, the stately form of Mont Cervin, or the Matterhorn, was also visible.

I shall never forget the beauty of that morning, from the moment when the first streak of dawn heralded the approach of the sun till he rose majestically above the horizon. The clear blue sky went through every gradation of colour, each seeming more lovely than the one by which it was preceded. It was a sky as impossible to describe as to forget.

At 6 A.M. I dismounted, for "Fritz" could go no farther, and I accompanied the gentlemen on foot the rest of the way, which is excessively steep. The path winds upwards amongst large blocks of stone, which form a kind of staircase to the summit. This I reached at 6.55 A.M., without once requiring any kind of assistance. At the top Mr. F___, who was the first to arrive there, offered his hand to assist me up the last few steps over the huge smooth blocks of stone of which the highest peak is composed, but I saucily declined the proffered help, as, had I accepted it, I should not have been able to say that I had ascended without assistance. This I was anxious to do, for Murray, speaking of the Aeggisch-horn, says, "This is a new expedition, just beginning to be known, and is a fatiguing day for ladies; few would attempt to climb the horn, and indeed the view is not so greatly superior to that from the lower ridge as to make it essential to incur the additional fatigue." In this opinion I do not at all concur; for I not only climbed up, but also came down again, without any other aid than that of my trusty Alpen-stock and the occasional assistance afforded by my taking hold of the rocks on the side of the path. I must also add that, to my taste, the view from the summit of the horn is so immeasurably superior to what can be seen from below, that no one ought to be content with the view from the lower ridge who has strength to climb for an hour, and has a head steady enough to enjoy the view from this surprising pinnacle. On reaching the summit, one's first difficulty is to discover a secure resting-place from which to make observations, for there is no level spot on which to stand; but having done this, I found myself poised on a pile of huge, loose rocks, which are heaped together on the top of the mountain in so strange a fashion that one wonders the heap does not separate and tumble down on the Aletsch Glacier below. This feeling of insecurity is however soon forgotten, and the mind becomes absorbed in admiration and delight at the wonderful view. This is almost unparalleled in extent and variety. It embraces the range of the Bernese Alps on the north, and that of the Monte Rosa chain on the south. The Aeggisch-horn is placed between these two magnificent chains of mountains, and at an immense depth below, at one's very feet, lies the great Aletsch Glacier, stretching away in an unbroken expanse for about twenty miles long and perhaps two or three wide. On the southern edge of this glacier is the small lake called

Märjelen See, which is of a deep blue colour, with icebergs of the purest white floating about in it. On every side arise snowy peaks of the highest mountains. . . .

We would gladly have spent several hours here, enjoying the magnificent panorama, and impressing its beauty more indelibly on our memories, but at 8 A.M. the mists began to rise from the valleys like steam, and soon interfered with the view, which had, till then, been uninterrupted. These mists rapidly increased, and hid from us all but occasional glimpses of the snowy chains which a few minutes before had been seen in the clear bright light of glorious sunshine. As soon as the mists reached and enveloped us, the air became very cold. Mr. F____'s Oberland guide, who was not well, had been trying for some time to shelter himself from the wind, and now looked so cold and wretched that we hastened to descend. At 8.30 A.M. we left the peak, and in an hour and a half descended to the inn. As we scrambled down the steep path we tried our voices against the abrupt precipices above us, and discovered several echoes with which we amused ourselves again and again, and we longed to have one of the famous buglers from the Lakes of Killarney—that paradise of harmonious echoes. At our *déjeuner* the landlord supplied, among other delicacies, a roast marmot, served hot. Its flavour is not wholly unlike hare, but the food is decidedly too rich for the digestion of ordinary mortals.

[1858]
We stayed for about a quarter of an hour at the châlets to rest, and took some slight refreshment before commencing the more arduous ascent which was to lead us to the Grivola. Not a glimpse of the Pic is to be obtained there, nor can it be seen at all until the Col is reached. The scene around us was one of singular wildness; on looking back we beheld the valley of Cogne at an immense depth below, but mists were driving rapidly through it, and curling up the sides of the mountains. Above us, on the right hand, towered an enormous buttress of rock, whose precipitous flanks appeared inaccessible, and which cut off from us all view of the Pic de Grivola, although we were in its immediate vicinity. Exactly in front of us, and below this rocky buttress, was a steep incline up which it was possible to go, but which was strewed over with masses of rock and débris that had fallen from the mountain above and formed that mixture of loose material which is so peculiarly undesirable for pedestrians.

On recommencing our journey I expressed my readiness to walk the rest of the way, but De la Pierre would not hear of it, and insisted that I could still ride "Nina" for half an hour longer. I accordingly remounted, and rode forwards. We then came to a large rock, which projects from the mountain and forms a small cave under it. Here I alighted, for the way up was getting too steep to allow me to ride farther with safety. The clouds, instead of dispersing, were becoming more dense, and our view was limited to occasional glimpses of the valley. We went a little farther, but a shower of rain-drops brought us to a sudden halt. De la Pierre and the chasseurs now assured us that we were only three quarters of an hour below the Col ascended by Mr. and Mrs. King, and from which they had enjoyed the magnificent view so eloquently described in "The Italian Valleys of the Pennine Alps." Under such circumstances we thought it was better to pause a little; for we had abundance of time before us, if the weather would only clear up. We therefore retreated to the huge rock I have just mentioned, and took shelter under it from the rain, which now began to assume a more decided character. Here we waited for more than two hours, amusing ourselves as well as we could. Dr. Argentier insisted that "Madame" must be provided with a suitable couch, and the chasseurs set to work, under his directions, to construct one. After much tugging and straining they succeeded in lifting into position a large flat slab of stone to form the seat; another slab was placed for the back, and a third, rather higher than the rest, for a pillow. The stony couch was then pronounced perfect, and "Madame" was requested to inaugurate it. I did so, and found it made a very comfortable seat—so comfortable indeed, that when I had been left quiet for a few minutes, I caught myself indulging in a slight nap after the fatigue of climbing. It was not possible, however, to enjoy much repose in the midst of such a merry band of companions; as the weather became worse, the jokes at our misfortune became more frequent, and we all tried to laugh away our disappointment with the best grace we could. Finding it utterly impossible to proceed farther on account of the rain, we determined to content ourselves with performing the civility of leaving our cards on La Grivola, as she was not visible to-day; accordingly slips of paper with our names written on them were deposited with great gravity in a broken bottle, and stowed away under the hospitable rock which had sheltered us.

All chance of the view was at last pronounced hopeless; the macintoshes were sent for, and thoroughly disheartened, we began our descent at 2.15 P.M. We went along at first slowly and reluctantly, with frequent backward glances in the direction we had wished to go, but had not proceeded far before the weather became worse, and it began to rain in torrents. There was then a regular scamper down the mountain, every one trying to run as fast as possible.

‹A scene of wild and striking grandeur»

Mrs. Freshfield Climbs the Titlis, 1859

In 1861, perhaps prompted by the success of *A Lady's Tour Round Monte Rosa*, Mrs. Cole's publisher brought out another mountain-travel book, this one entitled *Alpine Byways* and written, as the title page proclaimed, by "A Lady." In 1862, in the "lady's" second book, *A Summer Tour in the Grisons*, her name appeared as Mrs. Henry Freshfield. Freshfield was a member of an active and well-known mountaineering family (her son, Douglas, who made his first glacier crossing at the age of nine and who is referred to in the excerpt below as "D____," would go on to become president of both the Alpine Club and the Royal Geographic Society).

Mrs. Freshfield was probably a more ambitious alpinist than any other Englishwoman of her day. She generally climbed with her husband, her son, and a woman referred to below only as C____; her usual guide was Michael Alfonse Couttet, a relative of the Couttet who had guided Henriette d'Angeville on Mont Blanc. Like Mrs. Cole, Mrs. Freshfield insisted that "ladies may now enjoy the wildest scenes of mountain grandeur with comparative ease," and her books were quite influential—*A Summer Tour* is said to have set off a wave of summer tourism in the Engadine, leading to substantial development in that district. And though she claimed not to "aspir[e] to exploits which may be deemed unfeminine," she nonetheless made a number of notable ascents. In 1859, for example, she climbed the Schilthorn and crossed the Joch Pass before making the ascent, "rather an unusual one for ladies," of the 10,627-foot Titlis—an endeavour involving convoluted glaciers, steep ridges (or *arêtes*), and use of the climbing rope.

The excerpt below, reprinted from *Alpine Byways*, describes the Titlis climb. Whereas later accounts will focus more on the exigencies of the climbing itself, Freshfield, like Cole, still devotes much of her narrative to the view, sometimes described in terms (such as "stern grandeur") that were already becoming clichéd. Her tone is polite and reserved throughout, but we can still sense a note of satisfaction as she writes of the paucity of previous women climbers on the peak and the fact that, by day's end, the climb had proved more exhausting to her husband than herself.

WE KNEW NOTHING of the country between Meyringen and the upper end of the Lake of Lucerne, and our wish therefore was to cross the mountains by the Joch Pass, to Engelberg, and thence by the Surenen to Altorf.

It was not easy to gain information, but we learnt that a small inn, recently opened near the chalets of Engstlen, on this side the pass, would be decidedly the best resting-place; especially as we hoped to combine an ascent of the Titlis with our next day's journey. The distance to Engstlen was so easy (only five hours' ride), that we were tempted to indulge in breakfast at seven o'clock, and not to start for an hour later, when we found four good-looking and well-furnished horses in readiness, with two men to accompany them. The elder one professed to be well acquainted with the pass, and quite competent to act as guide to Engelberg. The young man did not know the way, but he seemed intelligent, and could understand and speak a little French; which was an advantage with Couttet, whose ignorance of German was often a difficulty in the Oberland, when arranging with the men. The heat was so great when we started, that we soon regretted the early hours which we had lost at Meyringen, especially as the road up the valley, as far as Imhoff, was exposed to the full glare of the sun. There we turned to the left, and had a very pretty ride, with an excellent road up the Gadmenthal. After crossing the river, and passing a most picturesque water-mill, we left the beaten path (which continues on, by the Susten Pass, to Wesen on the St. Gothard), and turning suddenly upwards, we gained the welcome shelter of a thick forest. The way was evidently very little used, and apparently no horses had passed this season, for the overhanging branches put our heads in jeopardy, and we soon dismounted, leaving the animals to clamber up the steep rocky staircases as best they could.

It was still early in the afternoon when we arrived at the inn, where we found all needful accommodation, with an intelligent and attentive landlord, who seemed anxious to merit the high recommendations bestowed on him in the "Travellers' Book." C_____ hoped to have spent an hour pleasantly in getting a sketch of the scene around, but another shower came on. The rest of the day was damp and gloomy, and we began to feel anxious about our journey the next morning. Our host was consulted about the necessary arrangements, and we were told that gentlemen often started to ascend the Titlis at one or two o'clock, A.M.! We had no fancy for crossing the Joch by the light of a lantern, so that suggestion was decidedly negatived; and finally it was arranged that, if the weather was favourable, we should be called at three o'clock.

The uncertainty was too exciting to allow us to sleep very soundly, and when I looked out at two o'clock, heavy clouds were scudding about, with mist driving over the mountains. We heard no sounds of preparation until past four, when we were told that appearances were improving. We finished dressing quickly, but the host assured us it was useless to hurry, and we waited, I fear not patiently, watching the Oberland range gradually coming into view. Summit after summit cleared, and as the wind came from that quarter, our hopes of a fine day strengthened, until at five o'clock it was thought prudent to start. Just as we mounted at the door of the inn, the Wetterhorn and its snow-capped neighbours caught the beautiful blush of early day, and this sight alone was worth the hour's delay in leaving Engstlen.

We found our party increased by two men, recommended by the landlord, whom Couttet had engaged as guides up the Titlis. The younger one carried ropes and a hatchet, preparations which gave D_____ great satisfaction, as showing that some real ice-climbing might be expected. The ascent is apparently rather an unusual one for ladies, and even while thus providing the necessary aid for our enterprise, I suspect that the good folks at Engstlen were somewhat incredulous as to its accomplishment.

In a few minutes we reached the margin of a lake, which the wet had prevented C_____ and myself from exploring the previous afternoon. The narrow path which we followed wound above it for about half-an-hour, rising gradually to the base of a steep ascent, with the snowy Titlis, now quite clear from clouds, full in view. The whole scenery was most striking in its stern grandeur, with rocky-crested summits frowning around us. Then the summit of the pass being gained, a splendid and extensive view of a new district, and combination of mountains, burst upon us, extending towards the Lake of Lucerne. Far beneath was another small lake, called the Trübsee; and near its further extremity, where some cattle looked like mice upon the pastures, the guide pointed out a solitary chalet, where travellers sometimes found very rough shelter for a night, before the Engstlen inn was opened. The men and horses from Meyringen were here to leave us, and they received directions to descend to a spot below the Trübsee (which the old man professed to know), there to await our return from the Titlis, no doubt existing that we should then gladly ride the remaining two hours' journey to Engelberg. Our party thus divided, we turned to the right, and had a rough scramble over rocks, followed by a short but rapid descent, in order to get across a bed of snow, apparently the remains of an avalanche. An alpine cry here awoke the mountain echoes, and we soon caught sight of two travellers, who proved to be an Englishman and his guide from Engelberg. Such meetings are always a pleasant excitement in these solitudes; and while a few words were interchanged we had time to admire the becoming costume of our countryman, quite à la Tyrolienne. Couttet (who found an acquaintance in the guide) told us that he had seen "Monsieur" last year at Chamouni, when he had ascended Mont Blanc. Now we climbed up steep pastures, crossed watercourses, and over soft loose shingle, until we reached a ridge of rocks, which projected into the valley, and descended in abrupt precipices on the other side. It was a magnificent position, immediately overlooking a vast glacier, with Engelberg almost lost in the depth below. The snowfield was still to be attained, with the summit far above shining clear and bright for our encouragement. After resting for a few minutes, we began the scramble up a very rough and steep arête, where some queer and precipitous rocky corners tested the steadiness both of head and feet. The mountain views on all sides were splendid, and called forth repeated exclamations of admiration as we advanced. Suddenly, amidst rugged desolation, affording no apparent sustenance for animal life, where one might have said—

"How bleak and bare it is—nothing but mosses
  Grow on these rocks,"

we were excited by seeing a hare start in front of us. After a moment's hesitation the frightened creature took its course upwards, and was quickly lost to us in the snow. After creeping very carefully round a slippery rock, we found ourselves on the verge of the glacier, with a yawning crevasse immediately in front, below which the icy stream descended rapidly towards the valley, ending in a grand row of glittering pinnacles. A slip in such a spot would be fatal; and we readily acquiesced in the prudence of using the ropes, which had been brought for such an emergency. The younger guide then led the way, followed by H____, our son, and myself, with Couttet's support between me and C____; the senior guide, who was very efficient, bringing up the rear.

We thus passed over an extensive snowfield, much intersected with crevasses, several of which we crossed on snow bridges. Then we reached the foot of a steep slippery brow, where the snow having melted had left an icy surface exposed, offering no possible foothold until the hatchet was used. The first guide therefore cut step by step as we advanced, and we soon found our upward progress comparatively easy. C____ ventured to suggest, "How are we to get down?" but it was better to postpone the consideration of that question until the time came. An unexpectedly [sic] difficulty now arose: my husband complained of feeling uncomfortable and rather faint, and when we again reached deep snow, through which the walking was really fatiguing, his breathing became oppressed and painful. What was to be done in such a dilemma? It was impossible to let him rest, and he would not listen to our proposal of returning, so, after a short delay, we continued our progress, but necessarily very slowly.

We gladly hailed a narrow ridge of rock, clear from snow, and fancied that the summit was just above us; but a deceitful hollow intervened, and there was yet another plunge through very deep snow; then all our energies were exerted for one more effort, and the highest point was gained. The sun shone brightly upon us, and fortunately the wind was neither high nor cold. We quickly arranged a resting-place for H____, where, sheltered by a cairn of stones, he soon revived after taking a little restorative, and was able to enter into our delighted enjoyment of the sublime scene around us. There was sufficient *brouillard* [fog] to obscure the distant horizon, but the panorama was magnificent; carrying the eye over ranges of mountain and grand glaciers, where

"Frost reigns everlastingly—and ice and snow
Thaw not."

Beyond the deep valley of Engelberg the Wallenstock and Uri
Rothstock were prominent amidst a wilderness of peaks, which intervened before a glimpse was gained of the Lake of Lucerne. To the left,
the Blankenstock and Schlossberg marked the line of the Surenen
Pass. On a perfectly clear day the view northward is said to extend to
Strasbourg Cathedral: this is a matter of faith, the truth of which we
had no opportunity of testing. To the east, the Alps of Glarus loomed
beyond the valley of the Reuss, bearing round to the St. Gothard,
beyond which the Galenstock rose above the glacier of the Rhone;
while nearer to us was the Süstenhorn, guarding the pass to Wesen.
The Oberland mountains were never clear, but presented ever-varying
forms of beauty as the drifting vapours constantly altered their position, and each snowy summit caught the sunshine.

"And many a pinnacle, with shifting glance,
Through the grey mist, thrust up its shatter'd lance."

The point on which we stood was dry and free from snow, which
enabled us to sit down and enjoy our luncheon while we watched the
clouds, which now began to gather together below, blotting out the
valley of Engelberg. It was a scene of wild and striking grandeur, very
different in character from the calm loveliness upon which we had
gazed from the Schilthorn.

Couttet, meantime, had made a discovery; and, much to our
amusement, he now presented me with the "Visitors' Book," which he
had found in a tin box stowed away in the centre of the stone pillar.
There were no entries of recent date, and lady visitors were apparently
not numerous. A pencil enabled us to add our names to the record, and
the book was then carefully restored to its hiding-place in the custody
of the "Steinmann."

The changing aspect of the weather at midday warned us not to
lengthen our stay; and, after spending an hour on the summit, we
turned to face the deep snow through which we must plunge. Soon we
were able to slide down more rapidly, and when we reached the steep
slope of ice, C____'s previous problem was quickly solved. The
younger guide took her in charge, and, holding her in a firm grasp,
commenced a glissade, which increased to such extreme velocity that
H____ looked on in perfect horror, almost expecting to see them both
disappear in a crevasse at the end of their career! The man, however,

knew well what he was about, as he proved when his pole escaped from his hand, and he threw himself cleverly down in front of C____, to stop her impetus until he could recover the pole. Then, looking triumphantly at the height from which they had descended, he said, very complacently, "Sie können sehr gut laufen" ["She found a good way"]. D____ and myself followed rather less rapidly, for at one time Couttet had us both in charge, and his care was great; but when, after depositing C____ safely on the snow field, the young man returned to us, D____ had the satisfaction of taking a downward flight under his wing. Thus we all descended merrily, and although the snow had become so moist and soft that we sunk in over our knees at almost every step, we reached the rocky *arête* in a quarter of the time which the ascent had occupied. We scrambled down and round the awkwardly-steep corners, often stopping to admire the grand glaciers and magnificent scene around. After resting a few minutes on the ridge, we should have finished the descent very easily, had we not found ourselves entering a dark cloud, which now hung like a canopy over the valley, and quite concealed Engelberg.

The old guide took leave of us about half way down, in order to return the same evening to his home at Engstlen. His companion was to remain until he had led us to the place where the horses were ordered to await us. Meanwhile, the mist grew thicker, and we heard distant mutterings of thunder, which reverberated among the mountains. Soon heavy drops fell, announcing the coming storm; then drenching rain and hail rattled on the umbrellas, with which we were fortunately provided. The footway led through spungy [sic] underwood, each track being a water-course, and we splashed along without much confidence in our route—the fog and hail making it very difficult to judge of the direction which we were taking. At last, when the storm cleared off, we found ourselves on a projecting knoll, overlooking the lake, where we ought to have received answers to the calls given in the expectation of discovering the retreat of the men and horses. Apparently they were neither within sight or sound. We began to fear that the stupid old man from Meyringen was again in fault, or that they must carelessly have missed the right place, and pursued the bridle way to a lower point, where it again intersects the footpath. There was no alternative but to send the Engstlen guide round to ensure our not leaving the horses behind us, while we continued the descent straight down a very steep and trying path, called the Pfaffenwand. This was an unwelcome addition to our walk, as regarded my husband, who seemed to have strained one of his knees, and nearly exhausted his powers. Couttet hastened on to seek tidings of the wanderers in the valley below, and we followed leisurely, congratulating ourselves that sunshine had succeeded the storm. Both C_____ and I were much too wet to induce us to mount, even if the horses appeared. We therefore decided, when we reached the meadows, to leave D_____ with his father, to await the result of the search, while we found our way on to Engelberg, and got things ready for their arrival. We had still a long half hour's walk before us, and the village was quite hidden by a steep wooded hill, beneath which it is situated. Fortunately we thus gained some shelter, for another shower came on. Our wet umbrellas had previously been given into Couttet's charge, and we made our *êntre* in somewhat ludicrous plight, with our cloaks over our heads and wet up to our knees.

The appearance of such "unprotected females" evidently created some surprise when we entered the hotel, and said we had come from the Titlis. When our dilemma was understood, the "Angel" and its inmates received us most hospitably, and the good people busied themselves most kindly in providing us with slippers and dry garments; indeed, I might have been fully equipped *à la Suisse* had all their hearty proffers been accepted. Happily there were rooms vacant, and we were just establishing ourselves comfortably, when H_____ and D_____ rode up, with attendants and baggage. After some difficulty the men had been discovered, comfortably reposing in a chalet, without any notion of looking out for our approach. Couttet was highly indignant at their conduct. . . .

«We *could* not give up»

Meta Brevoort Climbs the Bietschhorn, 1871

Like her British contemporary, Lucy Walker, the American Marguerite "Meta" Brevoort was one of the first women to spend her summers climbing seriously on a regular basis. She first visited Zermatt in 1865, just two months after the famous disaster that had claimed four lives on the pioneering ascent of the Matterhorn. With her was her fourteen-year-old nephew, William A. B. Coolidge, a chronically ill child she had brought along in the hope that the air of the Alps would prove healthful. The boy's health did improve dramatically, and he quickly came to share his aunt's love of mountain exercise. Their first climb together was the Cima di Jazzi, from which modest beginning the two would go on to form an accomplished climbing partnership.

Brevoort's great ambition was to be the first woman to climb the Matterhorn. She attempted the peak unsuccessfully in 1869, then in 1871 returned and succeeded—but was too late to claim the first ascent, for Lucy Walker had completed the climb just a few days earlier. Despite this bitter disappointment (or perhaps in part because of it), Brevoort later compiled an impressive record, including routes on the Monte Rosa, the Breithorn, the Jungfrau, the Finsteraarhorn, and—as she describes in the account below—the 12,970-foot Bietschhorn. She also made the first winter ascents of the Wetterhorn and the Jungfrau, climbs which marked the beginning of serious winter mountaineering by women.

Unlike the two previous excerpts, Brevoort's account is not a brief mountaineering interlude in what is otherwise a mountain-travel book, but instead is a consciously crafted story meant to stand on its own. It incorporates many of the elements that were then beginning to characterize the mountaineering essay as a distinct (if minor) genre: a brief resume of previous attempts on the peak, descriptions of the more exotic characters in the climbing party, a beautiful morning followed by deteriorating weather, and a harrowing descent that ends with a freezing night out in a storm. It was published in 1872 in the *Alpine Journal*, having been carefully written to conceal the author's sex (at one point she writes suggestively that the climbing party consisted of "a lady, myself," and several others) and then submitted under Coolidge's name—all to circumvent the *Journal*'s "men only" publication policy.

FIVE YEARS AGO, as we stood on the summit of the Nesthorn, we had gazed both admiringly and longingly at the Bietschhorn, whose magnificent outline and exquisitely-beautiful details form one of the most prominent features of that perfect view. At once we expressed a wish to attempt it, and were not a little disappointed at Almer's most discouraging reply that it was too *schwer* [difficult] for us. Though only too right, as we have since found out, he did not stick long to his opinion; so that for several years we had put down the Bietschhorn on our list of summer projects without ever having actually attacked it. Nor when we left Zermatt on the morning of the 18th of September 1871, did there appear to be much hope of our then accomplishing it. The weather seemed to have fairly gone to pieces. Dark and lowering from the first, we had not reached Randa before the rain began to come down in a gradually-increasing deliberate way, which gave no hope of mending for that day at least. So, as we jolted along in our rattling little conveyance, seeking for as much shelter as we could get from a huge red cotton umbrella, borrowed for us by the driver from some châlet on the road, we began recasting our plans to suit altered circumstances. . . .

I cannot say that we felt very despondent at the prospect of rest and ease which this change of plans implied, for we had been working very hard indeed for the past fortnight. Almer was equally inclined to view matters cheerfully, as he would now be able to visit a great cattle-fair at Meyringen, where he hoped to have an opportunity of buying "the last sweet thing" in the way of cows and pigs—a prospect seem-

Left to right: Christian Almer, William A. B. Coolidge, Marguerite "Meta" Brevoort, and Ulrich Almer, circa 1874. Photographer unknown. Courtesy of the Alpine Club Library.

ingly as charming to him as a day's shopping in Paris would be to most ladies. "And the Bietschhorn will be for next year;" and it seemed to float away dreamily with all the other "unvisited Yarrows" of our experience. At St. Nicolas we had to give up our little carriage, and being burdened with a tent and more baggage than the two Almers could conveniently carry, we took as porter to Visp the youngest of the three brothers Knubel, Peter Joseph by name, with whom we had only parted a day or two before. But as we journeyed on the weather began to show most decided symptoms of improvement. The rain ceased, the low hanging mist, which had hitherto enveloped the whole valley, as with a veil, gradually dispersed, the clouds broke away, and the sun shining out in the most brilliant mood imaginable, soon lent life, colour, and cheerfulness to the whole landscape. This was irresistible. We all agreed that it would be trifling with Fortune to slight such manifest kens of her favour; and giving up all thoughts of inglorious ease and fat cattle, the Bietschhorn again became our motive and hope.

Next morning was beautiful, and as we gazed upwards at our peak, which just showed its summit above the darkly-wooded hills which wall in the valley, we longed to be off at once; but one of our party being a slow walker, and the days already very short, we knew it would be impossible to reach the top at any decent hour unless we started from some higher point than the inn. The first day's walk would necessarily be a short one, as we could go no farther than the base of the mountain, and there pass the night in a tent, setting off early the next morning.

As there was no use in leaving Reid before noon, we amused ourselves with looking over the "livre des voyageurs," and in trying to make out, as well as we could with an imperfect knowledge of German, the account given in the Swiss "Jahrbuch" for 1869–70 by M. de Fellenberg of his ascent of our mountain. Whether it was that we did not arrive at the true meaning of the text, or that we were in a very reckless and absurd frame of mind, I know not; but there were parts of the narrative which made us shout with laughter, although I think they were intended to excite very different feelings in the reader. From it we gathered that at one time the luckless narrator and his companions were obliged to descend an arête literally *à califourchon* [by straddling]. Instead of compassionating their most uncomfortable position, a spirit of madness seized us, and we laughed till we were tired as we imagined them. But "rira bien qui rira le dernier" [who laughs last, laughs best] proved a true proverb in our case, for the time came when we fully realized what the difficulties of that same ridge were, and when they no longer affected our risible faculties. Meanwhile, unconscious of our approaching doom, we laughed, feeling quite positive that *we* should never ascend or descend in that fashion.

Our host looked as if he had once seen a ghost, and had never quite recovered from his fright. He really was so devoted to our comfort that we felt quite grateful to him, until he informed us that he made no money at all by his inn, and kept it from purely philanthropic motives. After that, we considered him as only following a strong natural vocation for hospitality—in fact, a sort of lay monk of the order of St. Bernard on a mission in the wilderness of the Lötschthal. He appeared to think that we must feel hungry every half-hour, and was constantly coming in to propose some new kind of refreshment, as well as to report progress concerning the provisions being got ready below; and thus let us into the secret of the "wildness," if one may so call it, of his larder. It was the result of the hunting propensities of a very profitable lodger he was entertaining for the summer, who spent all his time in the woods shooting, accompanied by a curious dumb dog, whose acquaintance we also made. This dog could not bark, and wore a bell that his master might know his whereabouts. As our dog Tschingel, who was with us, came originally from the Lötschthal, and very much resembled our new friend (except in his dumbness), we tried to persuade him to fraternise with one who was probably some near connection; but Tschingel indignantly repudiated the theory, and showed the most worldly-wise contempt for his poor relation, not suffering him to enter the dining-room. We were also much interested, and indulged in sundry speculations as to the origin and history of a very ancient pike and part of a suit of armour, both of gigantic size, which our host told us had been found in a neighbouring village, while clearing away the ruins of some cottages which had been burnt down. A dagger, found at the same time, and of equally wonderful proportions, he had given, he said, to M. de Fellenberg.

At noon we set off—a funny-looking party. Christian and Ulrich Almer carried the ropes and provisions, Knubel the tent, Siegen some blankets, a Ried porter a *hotte* [container] full of nondescript articles for the cuisine; and, lastly, an Oberlander, who had asked Almer to employ him, was loaded with a huge bundle of straw, which made him look like a walking haystack, and which was intended for those who were to sleep outside the tent. Nothing could be more beautiful in its way than was our walk to the camping-place. After crossing the little stream in front of the inn, and going through some meadows, we entered the most solemn old pine-woods. The brilliant sunshine which streamed here and there through their sombre branches dispelled all gloom, but could not banish the feeling of quietness and mystery peculiar to them. We were sorry to leave their shade for steep, stony grass-slopes. The men here began to gather firewood as they strolled along. We climbed slowly, looking back continually at the various new peaks now showing themselves on the opposite side of the valley. Among these the Breithorn was conspicuous, and the broad, level summit of the Petersgrat became plainer every moment. Siegen and the Ried porter, who was his servant, soon showed symptoms of fatigue, and were continually suggesting that it was time to set up the tent, as, if we went too far, it might be inconvenient to get water.

Almer lent a deaf ear for a long while to all their remarks, until we had got on to the lower end of the great rocky mass which divides the Nest and Birch glaciers, and culminates in a point marked 3,320 on the Federal map. Here he proposed that we should halt, whilst he pushed on alone to reconnoitre. Away he went, climbing up some very steep rocks in his usual rapid manner, and was soon out of sight. This seemed a favourable opportunity for examining Siegen with more attention than we could give him whilst walking. And he really was worth inspection, somewhat resembling one of Salvator Rosa's brigands, but still more the conventional stage representation of Mephistopheles. His dark eyes, heavy eyebrows, long black hair, and still longer moustaches, with that peculiar twist in them remarkable in those of the chief personage in "Faust," were most picturesquely set off by a slouched hat, ornamented with a long trailing bunch of cock's feathers. It was impossible not to attempt a sketch of him, and to this he lent himself very complacently, recounting the while various details of M. de Fellenberg's ascent, and dwelling especially on the really amazing quantity of wine he had helped to consume on that occasion. We were much edified, when, as he pulled out his handkerchief, two or three sets of beads came out with it, which, he laughingly said, were none too many for the Bietschhorn.

In about an hour Almer returned, having found exactly the place for our camp; and, much to Siegen's regret, we all set off to reach it, and arrived there at 4 P.M., the whole ascent from Reid, with numerous halts, having only occupied 3-1/2 hours. The two porters were sent back somewhat later. Our position was a commanding one. Looking back towards Reid (which we could not actually see), the Nest glacier was on our left, far below us, the rocks on which we were standing rising very precipitously above it. On our right were wild savage cliffs, which rose higher and higher behind us, until, far above, we could see the sharp summit of our peak looking down upon them. It seemed almost to beckon us on to attempt it, as it shone out gloriously in the light of the setting sun, the rays of which made the snowy range on the opposite side of the valley glow with new beauty. In the midst of this splendid scene, and after a much-enjoyed supper, we retired to rest, full of hope for the morrow, though somewhat chilled by the cold September night air.

The night proved sharp and frosty, and we did not start the next morning till after 5.30 A.M., when the sun had gained a little strength. The party consisted of a lady, myself, the two Almers, Knubel, and

Siegen. It was thought best to leave Tschingel, our faithful dog, behind in the tent, *not* because of any supposed incapacity on his part, as he [according to Cicely Williams, Tschingel was actually female] was perhaps the most accomplished mountaineer of the party, but because Almer feared that he would throw down stones from above upon us, as he always chooses his own route on the ascent and insists upon leading.

We began at once to climb the steep rocks immediately behind our camp, and at 6.50 A.M. got on to the Nest glacier, near a large cave or hole formed by the rocks overhanging the glacier at their point of junction, on the side of the rocky mass mentioned above. With this cave, which we scarcely noticed at the time, we afterwards became rather intimately acquainted. Mounting the glacier gradually, meeting with a few crevasses, we soon reached the centre of the semicircle plainly visible on the map, and at the very foot of the mountain, which we now saw for the first time from tip to toe, being even able to distinguish one of the stone men on the summit.

It may not be out of place here to give a slight sketch of the peak of the Bietschhorn. It is formed by the union of three principal arêtes, running roughly towards the north, south, and west. The summit is a long and extremely shattered ridge, out of which rise three rocky towers, nearly equal in height. The southern arête falls away precipitously towards the valley of the Rhone, but the two others are more practicable. Mr. Leslie Stephen, when he made the first ascent of the mountain, in 1859, seems to have followed the northern arête on his ascent and descent. When the mountain was climbed for the second time, in 1867, by M. de Fellenberg, the ascent was effected, I believe, by the western, and the descent by the northern arête. Several attempts to ascend the peak failed, and ours was the next successful ascent. As will be seen, we exactly reversed M. de Fellenberg's route.

It was after 7.30 A.M. when we halted for breakfast in the centre of the semicircle mentioned above, after which repast we parted with Siegen, who showed no unwillingness to return to the tent, Knubel having petitioned to be allowed to go to the top, and Almer thinking that as Ulrich was also with us we could very well dispense with Mephistopheles. Turning to the left, our party of five marched over the glacier to the base of the northern arête, which we began slowly to ascend. The rocks were very rotten, and fell down at the slightest touch, so that we had to be very cautious in our movements. We gained the crest of the arête, after a good deal of trouble, at 10.30 A.M., and followed it henceforth, with slight deviations, to the summit. It very soon turned into a very sharp snowridge, which had a threatening corniche overhanging the Jägifirn of the Federal map. The weather up to this time had been perfect, and whenever we could afford the time, we had been only too glad to pause and gaze at the magnificent prospect which began to unfold itself before us. But now a change came over the fair scene. A strong icy wind began to whistle about our ears, and rising clouds to surround us. The ridge along which we were cautiously stepping was already quite difficult enough, without this most unpleasant companion, and now became utterly impracticable. Abandoning it, therefore, for a while, we crept along the projecting rocks just below it, overhanging the Nest glacier, until it became somewhat wider, and we were able once more to return to it. But the snow here turned into ice, and many a weary step had to be cut before the first stone man was reached at 12.30 P.M. The wind was still howling and nipping our noses, ears, and fingers pitilessly; but, although there was now no hope of a view, we *could* not give up our summit. It was with difficulty that we made our way along the shattered ridge, trying, whenever we could, to keep below it. At length we reached the top at 1.10 P.M., the ascent having occupied 7-1/2 hrs., including all halts. We could see nothing beyond the rocks immediately around us, as we were enveloped in clouds, which the wind drove about tumultuously. But, although we regretted the magnificent prospect from the top, we were struck with the grandeur of what we could see—jagged rocks, splintered into every conceivable shape, piled up or strewn out in fantastic confusion. The drifting clouds also enabled us occasionally to form some idea of the startling precipices on all sides.

After a very slender and hurried repast, we turned to descend at 1.30 P.M., leaving our names in a bottle, carefully placed in the cairn. It was shortly after that a startling sight greeted us. The sun was glaring through the clouds, like a smouldering ball of fire. Suddenly we perceived a rainbow around us, and in the space between it and the sun our shadows were distinctly projected. It was almost unearthly to see these figures of gigantic proportions moving as we moved.

We had now got back to the first stone man, and the clouds were becoming more broken every moment, so that there was a chance of our being seen in the valley. We therefore tied an old red handkerchief, which our host at Reid had asked us to use as a flag, to a stick, which was planted in the cairn, and was in a few minutes distinctly seen at Reid and at Kippel. We had no time to spare, and I rather believe the unexpressed wish of each of us was to get safely down again.

According to our original plan, we were to have descended direct to Raron, between Turtmann and Visp in the Rhone valley, at the opening of the Bietsch Thal—a route which some of us still think would have been the best to adopt. Siegen, however, had so opposed it, that Almer had given it up before starting. We then determined to return the same way by which we had ascended. That way, however, had proved so dangerous towards the top, that Almer, with his usual prudence, altered our course. The upper part of the western arête being impracticable, he therefore led us down the great rock couloir, which opens out near the first cairn, and is well shown on the Federal map, being the space between the western arête and a spur of the southern. It was very steep, and the rocks, as everywhere else on this mountain, were of the most treacherous and unstable description, with no fixed principles to speak of. Almer meant, after descending this couloir for some distance, to mount to the right, in order to gain the crest of the arête, and to descend by the northern face to the Nest glacier—an excellent plan, had it not proved impracticable, owing to the many little ridges which shot out from the main ridge, and had every one to be crossed to gain the crest at a practicable point. At first we were very cheerful about it, expecting every one of these contradictory obstacles to be the last, but no sooner had we surmounted one than another cropped up before our disappointed eyes, and we began to lose patience. It would have been bearable, of course, however fatiguing, had we had any time to spare, but the light was fast fading, and, hurry as much as we could, we felt that night was approaching without any sign of a deliverance. So here we were, *we* who had felt so confident that we should never follow M. de Fellenberg's route, descending the very way he went up! And such rocks as they were! In the morning there had been some pretence at cohesion, owing to the night's frost, but now they had only too completely recovered their independence. They rolled down if one did but look at them. One immense fragment suddenly broke loose from a ledge which we had just descended, and falling on the rope between Almer, who was leading, and his immediate follower, dragged them both off their feet. They went rolling over and over, pulling down Ulrich, who came next, so that the three executed several prodigious somersaults before they were stopped by the last two of the party. The rope was found to be

almost cut through where the boulder had struck it. A second occur-
rence of the kind, only a little less alarming, followed soon after; and
what with Almer's continual "Geben sie acht," "Dieses ist nicht fest,"
"Dieses ist ganz locker" [take care—these aren't solid], and the continual rattling of stones about us, we became quite bewildered, and
began at times to fancy that the whole mountain was coming down
about our ears like a card-house. The twilight was fading away when
we crossed the last little ridge, and at length set foot on the arête at its
extreme western end. The moon had risen, but our old enemy, the
wind, which had never ceased to blow, drove the clouds over her face,
only allowing us occasional faint glimmers of light as we stumbled
along, with many a fall on the cruel hard rocks, which, touch them
never so lightly with foot or hand, set off at once with an avalanche of
smaller stones in their wake. At length, bruised, weary, and sleepy, we
reached the snow-field forming the summit-level of the Bietsch joch at
8.20 P.M., after a most painful descent of 6-1/4 hrs., the like of which
we had never experienced, and hope never to experience again. The
wind had now completely buried the moon in a bank of clouds, and
the only light we had was that of a faintly-twinkling star or two. This
mattered little so long as we were on the snow, through which we
plunged rapidly, keeping to the right, until in 25 minutes we arrived at
the exact spot where we had breakfasted in the morning. We knew
this, because we here found a precious little barrel of wine, left buried
in the snow, the recovery of which we had been for some time antici-
pating, as we had had nothing to drink since quitting the summit.

After this our difficulties began again. The glacier which still lay
between us and the rocky mass, on the lower part of which stood our
tent (our tent!), which had become to us the very embodiment of
home comforts and safety, had been traversed without much difficulty
in the morning, but to descend it in almost total darkness was a very
different thing.

We groped along after Almer, who guided himself in a wonderful
manner, occasionally even recovering for a few minutes our morning's
track by feeling with his hands for the steps cut in the ice, literally
going à tâtons [feeling his way]! Whenever we came to a crevasse,
Ulrich sat down, and held his father by the rope, that he might creep
over to find a safe way, and then direct us how to follow him. It was of
course impossible, even with his consummate skill, to make rapid
progress, and indeed we could not tell that we were not going backward instead of forward. We lost all hope of getting off the glacier for

the night, but it was so bitterly cold that Almer would not allow us to make any halt, fearing lest we should freeze. A pleasant prospect this, of creeping almost on all fours about a glacier, with the wind whistling around us in the most derisive manner! Now and then the men would speak to one another, and in the midst of the incomprehensible patois gibberish which they always adopt on trying occasions, we could hear the word "loch," and remembered a cave at the edge of the glacier which we had passed in the morning. It seemed so utterly improbable that we should ever find it again, that we gave no thought to the subject. What, then, was our delight when Almer exclaimed (this time in comprehensible German) that he felt sure that we were near that cave. Untying himself, he went off to reconnoitre, and joyfully called out to us to follow his track, as he had found it. It showed how closely he must, on the whole, have kept to the straight road, that in spite of occasional wanderings, we actually came out at the *very* place where we had taken to the ice in the morning. It was entirely due to his marvelous skill and sagacity that we did not spend the night on the ice. It was not a few minutes past 11 P.M., as we found out by striking one of a few precious matches which we had brought. Our tent was not very far off, but we were too thoroughly tired out to think of any more scrambling down the rocks which lay between us and it. So we thankfully descended one by one into the cave, which was large enough to contain us all, though not the most comfortable of places. However, we were only too glad of the shelter which it afforded us from the cold wind which howled outside, and too delighted to be off the ice and able to sit down to complain of anything. We had no more provisions, not having expected to be out so long, so that the satisfaction of eating was denied to us. We still had a very little wine, but that little was in a spiteful cask, out of which it was very difficult for an unpractised person to drink, and pouring it out into a leather cup in the dark was altogether too wasteful a process. Matches were now and then struck to find out the time. In spite of cold, hunger, and discomfort, we would drop off to sleep for a few minutes; but whenever a dead silence showed this to be the case, Almer would jump up and begin yodelling in the most aggravating manner, or else he would circulate the hateful little cask, addressing us in the liveliest manner, and thus to our disgust effectively rousing us up from our slumbers, which the cold rendered very dangerous.

Before daylight the wind ceased and snow began to fall. We were not able to leave the hospitable hole till nearly 5 A.M., after a stay of

6 hrs. We then followed our previous day's route down the rocks, amid the falling snow, and regained the tent at 6.30 A.M. Siegen came to greet us with a bottle of champagne, provided by our philanthropic host, for which we heartily blessed him. The thoughtful man had sent up two porters to the tent, to find out what had become of us; and seeing us afar, they lit a great fire, the very sight of which was cheering on that wintry-looking morning. Tschingel, who had threatened to devour poor Siegen when he first tried to enter the tent on his return the day before, and was only pacified by the most abject advances from him, gave us an uproarious welcome. The kettle soon boiled, and we had some hot tea and coffee, after which we took a good rest in the tent, and descended to Reid in rain later on in the day. Our host received us with the choicest hospitality in his power—a dish of brains for dinner.

Thus ended an adventure which was not far from having a serious end, since, in all probability, had we spent the night on the ice, this paper would never have been written.

«A tie on one's conscience»

Emily Hornby Climbs the Titlis, the Nuvolao,
and the Monte Cristallo, 1873–88

Emily Hornby's climbing and traveling career spanned a period of at least twenty years, but as a climber she was neither well known nor at the cutting edge of the sport. Unlike her more famous predecessors, who typically climbed in the company of a male relative, or at least with a long-term guide who was so trusted and familiar as to be virtually a member of the family, Hornby appears to have ranged widely on her own, engaging guides on an ad hoc basis as she moved from one Alpine center to another and frequently climbing with women she met in her travels—a casual approach to alpinism made possible by improved access to the mountains, the steadily increasing numbers of travelers visiting them, and, perhaps, by the more relaxed social codes of the later Victorian era. Certainly the fact that Hornby could have climbed so many peaks—the Jungfrau, the Matterhorn, the Eiger, and some thirty-five others—and yet remain relatively unknown indicates that women climbers were no longer a novel sight in the Alps.

The excerpts below are reprinted from *Mountaineering Records*, a collection of Hornby's letters and journals edited and published in 1907 by her sister, M. L. Hornby. Not originally intended for publication, these entries are spontaneous and personal if not polished. They reveal Hornby as a climber occasionally concerned with setting records, anxious to compare her performance with that of others or to know how many women climbers may have preceded her. At other times she seems sim-

ply to enjoy (and in one case not to enjoy) the experience of
climbing itself.

ENGELBERG, *August 7th*, 1873. That afternoon I went up to the Trübsee
hut to sleep to be ready for Titlis next day, it is eight hours to the top
from here, so I thought it better to divide it, and up to the Trübsee it is
very steep and stony. It had been such lovely weather hitherto I never
thought of rain, but all night long there was an awful thunderstorm
with deluges of rain, and next morning a thick fog, so I came down
again, thoroughly depressed. After that, Titlis was enveloped in clouds
for two or three days, but about Tuesday it began to clear, and I fixed to
try again, Hilda [an American met at Engelberg] having announced
she should like "to go along" we set off together with a guide apiece,
and got very successfully to the Trübsee by daylight. It was pitch dark
when I got there the time before, and I left it in fog, so I had no idea
what it was like—a lovely little grassy basin, the snow close down all
round. The first time I had it all to myself, but this time it was very
different, Hilda and I had to sleep together in one bed, and a little boy
and girl from Basle together in the other, it was very funny. We were
roused before twelve, and had to start at half-past with lanterns, and
for three hours had to go on stumbling and tumbling in pitch darkness:
I could not see at all, Hilda managed much better. I was thankful when
it began to dawn, I thought it never would. We had a halt at dawn
under a large rock, and some food, and then started again, now we had
light, and a splendid sunrise. When we got to the glacier we were roped
together, the glacier was most easy to cross, but afterwards we had a
steep slope of very slippery snow with no footing at all. We struggled
up breathless, and it was fortunately not very long, and afterwards it
was not so steep, and there was more footing. It was bliss when we saw
the cairn at the top, and we finally got there soon after seven, six hours
and a quarter from the Trübsee. I am sure I should have been nearly an
hour less about it but for the darkness. Five and a half hours is the time
given in Baedeker, so it was only three quarters of an hour more after
all. It was a splendid panorama view, but nothing, in my mind, to the
one from the Schilthorn. It was awfully cold, but we found a sheltered
nook, where we had some food with the little boy and girl from Basle,
who, I regret to say, had got up half an hour before us. There is a book
in the cairn where we wrote our names, but I could not find any trace
in it of F. or O. or E. and P. Coming down over the snow was great fun,

I pulled Hilda down several times [by the slack unexpectedly going out of the climbing rope], and kept up myself very well, I was glad, as I had tumbled going up more than she did. We got down in five hours, the last hour from Engelberg down what they call the Pfaffenwand is awfully steep, and it was very hot, and poor Hilda quite gave in and fainted. I was on in front, and did not know till she came up to me again, leaning on her guide's arm. I was quite fresh, only boiled and rather footsore. I always get so footsore just the last hour or two down, which are always over rough stones. Hilda retired to bed at once (one o'clock), and did not appear till the same hour next day. I need not say I went about as usual, and was very thankful for Speis. I let H. read this and she thinks I shall have given you the idea that I pulled Hilda down on purpose, because she went up better than I did. It was her own fault letting the rope get tight between us, the guide in front would have pulled me down if I had let him get it tight, but of course I did not.

HOTEL MONTE ROSA, ZERMATT, *August 6th*, 1881. There has only been one bad day since I left home the 4th July, and that day I was walking down a long valley, and was quite thankful to have rain instead of sun. I have been successful this tour beyond my wildest dreams, till yesterday, when a thing happened to me which has never happened before. I had started on Thursday for the Dom, one of the Mischabel Hörner near here. I knew it to be long and tiresome, but of no particular difficulty, but being the highest mountain in Switzerland I wanted to have done it. I got to the sleeping-place on the rocks all right on Thursday, and yesterday started for the top, and somehow could not get on. The weather was splendid, the glacier in very nice order, but the rocks too dreadful, either all the crumbly stuff, Geröll, or very sharp points cut into layers. I never saw such odd rocks. I toiled and toiled, and never seemed to get on, and I thought of giving in, a thing I never did before. At last the thought of giving in began to be pleasant to me, and I asked them frankly, going on as I was going then, how long did they think I should be? One said three hours, and the other did not think three hours would do it. I then quite decided to give in, I felt I could not bear three hours more, and I did not even care to go on, I never felt like that before. I should have been wild on either the grand Paradis or the Matterhorn at the thought of turning back, and generally I go plodding on without thinking of time. So we did turn back and I don't much care, even to-day. Anderegg, my own guide, is perfectly miserable, he never ceases saying "Ach, es ist grosse Schade; Es thut mir sehr Leid!" [It's a great pity]. It is a fearful tie having a perpetual guide, and I shall never have one again. It was so delightful last year in the Tyrol being rid of them between times and not having them always loafing about, a tie on one's conscience when one wants to be quiet. It was very well we did turn back yesterday, for, as it was, we only got to our sleeping place by seven o'clock, these horrid rocks took almost as long to come down as to go up, and the glacier was still more crevassed, one had to be going round to get out of the way. This morning we had come down to Randa, we started at 4.30 and were there before nine, I had some food, drove back here, and was dropped at the baths. . . . I propose on Tuesday going over the Mischabel Joch to Saas, and from there to the Eggischhorn. . . . The hotel is so full to-day, being Saturday the people come here for church. There is a concert in another hotel this evening at eight. I shall feel obliged to go as the proceeds are to be given to the poor at Zermatt, though I would much rather have gone to bed. I have done the Mont Pourri this year, which I believe no female has done, and also crossed the Grand Paradis from Cogne to Val Savaranche, which also I don't believe any female has done. . . . On the other hand all the female mountaineers have done the Dom, and I never heard it thought much of, I cannot think what possessed me, but it cannot be helped.

AQUILA NERA, CORTINA, *July 30th*, 1886. The weather is now lovely, and Cortina so very delicious I am staying longer than I intended. I had a hard day yesterday, and am only prowling about. I went up the Nuvolao yesterday. It is a minor Dolomite, in a very central position, and the view was certainly splendid, and most of the more famous Dolomites were quite close. I started at four in the morning, and the sunrise reflected on Monte Grace was quite splendid; it looked scarlet. The Nuvolao has two points—the higher one difficult and the lower one easy. I did the difficult one first; it had only one bad place, but that really was most awkward. I almost thought at one moment I should have had to give in. The guide first scrambled up a sort of flat face of rock where there seemed no footing at all, and then I had to work myself up a sort of chimney to get to the point where he was—I could not possibly have got up the flat face. There was no footing at all in the chimney, and I had to worm myself up till I could get on my knees on a flat stone, and I kept getting my head under this stone, and could not get beyond it. I lost my hat and the net off my hair, but at last accomplished it. I had previously lost a red shawl, and the skirt of my dress was left intentionally below—so that the Nuvolao was strewed with my property. They were all recovered except the net. When we got to the top we saw another party making their way up—a lady on a mule—and their guide began shouting to mine; they wanted to come up too, but had no rope. They had picked up my red shawl. We were altogether an hour-and-a-half at the top, it was so delightful; then got down, which was rapidly accomplished. My guide ran off to these other people with the rope, and then I went to the lower point—rather grudging the trouble, for it took nearly an hour. Soon after we got there we had the amusement of looking at the other people on the point, and when we had got down they had just got to the bad place coming down, so we sat and watched them. I could just make them out, and I knew they were English, for I distinctly heard the lady call out, "All right." They did not overtake us on the way down, though I sat half-an-hour at a delicious little inn about an hour above Cortina, having coffee; but at dinner I found I was sitting next them—a very nice man and his niece. They had never thought of going on that point till they saw me, and then they thought they must.

AQUILA NERA, CORTINA, *August 4th*, 1888. I found your letter yesterday on my return from Monte Cristallo. It was the great thing I wanted to accomplish this tour. I was baulked of it two years ago by bad weather. . . . I almost think I prefer this place to San Martino, there is much more variety in the way of walks. . . . We stayed two days at Pieve di Cadore, which is a most exquisite place. I at once began taking steps about a guide, and was very glad to secure the one I had when I was here before, and another very good one. On Friday evening, about six, I started for the little inn at the top of the Tre Croci pass, about an hour-and-a-half from here. It was very cold and they had been scouring all the rooms, and they were sopping wet. I thought I should get rheumatism but have not. I went to bed wrapped in all my out-door clothes, and should have slept very well, only on those occasions I am so nervous about not being called I strike a match about every hour to see what time it is. The Italian guides are much more prompt at starting than the Swiss, who are ages getting ready. We were off at three next morning, and at the top at 10.30, and never, not even on the Italian side of the Matterhorn, had I such a scramble. I had to be constantly worming myself up chimneys of rocks, the sides all ice, there were the largest icicles I ever saw. At the top all was clouds, but I had beautiful peeps going up and down, and the rocks of Cristallo were a sight to behold, perfectly perpendicular smooth red walls of an immense height. Cristallo itself is most beautifully jagged at the top, I thought we should never get to the real top. There was a visitor's book in a tin box under a rock at the top. I did not see the name of any English female but there were three Germans, one of them Madame Tenschker, with whom I was once in the Concordia hut.

«Suitable to the weaker sex»

Mary Mummery
Climbs the Teufelsgrat of the Täschhorn, 1887

Mary Mummery began her Alpine climbing in the 1880s, after she married Albert Frederick Mummery (famous for his first ascent of the notoriously difficult rock peak, the Grépon). In her first season she made an impressive start, climbing the Jungfrau and the Matterhorn. A more difficult climb—and one that, as she lets us know in the excerpt below, had been considered beyond women's ability—was the Teufelsgrat, the hitherto unclimbed "devil's ridge" of the 14,758–foot Täschhorn. This came at a time when most of the major Alpine peaks, including the Täschhorn, had already been climbed by their easiest slopes, prompting the more elite climbers to test their skills (and maintain their status) by attempting more difficult routes.

Mummery was not the first woman to participate in such a difficult first ascent, but she seems to have been the first to insist publicly that women might prove better suited to such challenging climbs than the comparatively tame ascents to which they were generally relegated. In doing so she cleverly argues for women's ability by appealing to contemporary notions of women's *debility*: women can more easily keep pace with supposedly more athletic men on climbs so steep and technically difficult they require *everyone* to proceed slowly.

In the account below, published in 1896 as a chapter in Albert's *My Climbs in the Alps and Caucasus*, Mummery sustains an ironic tone that gives her work a bite lacking in the preceding selections. For example, her remarks on the "masculine

Mary and Albert Mummery and child. Photographer unknown. Courtesy of the Alpine Club Library.

mind" and on boastful, chauvinistic "mashers" are humorous enough, though obviously intended to make her readers think as well as laugh.

THE SLOPES of the Breithorn and the snows of the Weiss Thor are usually supposed to mark the limit of ascents suitable to the weaker sex—indeed, strong prejudices are apt to be aroused the moment a woman attempts any more formidable sort of mountaineering. It appears to me, however, that her powers are, in actual fact, better suited to the really difficult climbs than to the monotonous snow grinds usually considered more fitting.

Really difficult ascents are of necessity made at a much slower pace, halts are fairly frequent, and, with few exceptions, the alternations of heat and cold are less extreme. Snow grinds, on the contrary, usually involve continuous and severe exertion—halts on a wide snow field are practically impossible—and the danger of frost-bite in the early morning is succeeded by the certainty of sun-burning at mid-day.

The masculine mind, however, is, with rare exceptions, imbued with the idea that a woman is not a fit comrade for steep ice or precipitous rock, and, in consequence, holds it as an article of faith that her climbing should be done by Mark Twain's method, and that she should be satisfied with watching through a telescope some weedy and invertebrate masher being hauled up a steep peak by a couple of burly guides, or by listening to this same masher when, on his return, he lisps out with a sickening drawl the many perils he has encountered.

Alexander Burgener, however, holds many strange opinions; he believes in ghosts, he believes also that women can climb. None the less it was with some surprise that I heard him say, "You must go up the Teufelsgrat." Now the Teufelsgrat, as its name implies, is a ridge of exceptional enormity, and one, moreover, that a few days previously, while we were ascending the Matterhorn, he had pointed out to me as the very embodiment of inaccessibility. I was proud of the compliment, and we solemnly shook hands, Burgener saying the while that the nominal proprietor of the ridge and all his angels should not turn us back, once we were fairly started.

For the benefit of those who may not be well acquainted with the Alpine possessions of his Satanic Majesty, it may be pointed out that the Teufelsgrat is the south-western ridge of the Täschhorn. A short distance north of the Täsch-Alp this ridge ends in the little peak called the Strahlbett. Our plan was to sleep at the Täsch-Alp and, crossing the Weingarten glacier, to climb up to a very obvious col immediately on the Täschhorn side of that small peak. From thence to the summit we hoped to be able to follow the ridge.

Burgener rejoiced in the approach of our first struggle, and could hardly restrain his exuberant spirits. He employed his time, when his mouth didn't happen to be more seriously occupied, by using his best English to try and shatter my nerves. He gave me various and most graphic pictures of the awful precipices which were to greet my inexperienced eyes, always ending each sentence with, "It is more beautifuls as the Matterhorn," that being the only peak we had previously ascended together.

Having exhausted the regulation time for feeding, the rope was got out and a business-like air settled on Burgener's countenance. He, of course, took the lead, I followed, then came Andenmatten, and my husband last. The rocks were fairly good for a little while, but as we got higher they became steeper and very rotten. Our leader took the greatest care not to upset any of the stones, and kept hurling frightful warnings at me to be equally careful. "You kill your man, you not like that!" I did not "kill my man," but, nevertheless, it was here that our first accident occurred.

We had reached a sort of platform cut off from the upper slopes by a precipitous wall of rock. At one point, however, where the end of an overlapping slab had weathered and decayed, it seemed just possible to surmount the barrier. Burgener was soon at work upon it, but the splinters of rock were so loose that no reliable grip could be found, and progress had to be made with foot and hand hold equally uncertain. Still he steadily advanced, and, at length, could just reach his hands over the top of the rock and clutch at a great stone which seemed firm. Firm it was to a certain extent. Firm enough not to roll over on our heads, but, alas! not firm enough to prevent a slight movement on to Burgener's hand. A stifled groan, a trickle of blood down the rocks, followed by a long and impressive sentence in patois, was all the intelligence vouchsafed us till, with a last effort, Burgener clambered on to the top of the wall. We quickly followed, and, finding a convenient ledge, proceeded to make our diagnosis. A somewhat mangled, swollen, and bleeding thumb offered an interesting problem to a student of the St. John's Ambulance Association. The bleeding was soon checked, and the offending thumb bound up in a variety of pocket-handkerchiefs, Burgener murmuring the while in most pathetic tones, "I no more strong in that hand."

We suggested an immediate retreat, but after a glance at the pinnacled ridge, now well within view, a half bottle of Bouvier (we had forgotten to bring any cognac) and a bite off the limb of a tough poulet, there issued from the invalid's lips sneering remarks at the idea of returning. "Vorwärts," he cried, and vorwärts we went, amidst a strange mixture of joyful yodels at the towering gendarmes which seemed to challenge us to wrestle from afar, and dejected looks and mournful voice repeating, "I no more strong in that hand."

About 5.30 A.M. we reached the ridge, here covered with snow. Andenmatten took the lead, and, as the snow was in excellent condition, we were able to make good pace. This was soon succeeded by queer, slabby, stratified rocks, piled at a steep angle, like rows of huge slates, one on the other. Their sharp edges, however, offered good hold for hands and feet. After a short time these broken rocks were interspersed with an occasional bold, precipitous turret, forcing our leader to show his metal. This first gendarme was, nevertheless, successfully passed, and the second stood before us—a large, piled-up mass of brownish yellow, rotten rock, blocking entirely from our view the rest of the arête.

After a short consultation between the guides the best route was singled out, and Andenmatten once more advanced to the attack. The base of the tower went well, and little by little the difficulties seemed to be yielding. Our leader's face beamed with pride and pleasure, as he stormed crag after crag, but, alas! he forgot the well-worn proverb, "Pride goeth before destruction, and a haughty spirit before a fall."

Solomon was once more to be justified, and the joyful Andenmatten was to be the victim. A last small, rocky tooth impeding his progress, and not being able to find sufficient hold, he summoned Burgener to his aid. The suggestion that he should take off the knapsack was treated as an insult, and a minute later, aided by a friendly shove, he had not merely got good hold on the top of the tooth, but was actually resting his arms on it. The tooth was to all intents and purposes climbed, when, to our horror, we saw his arms sliding off, and with a last convulsive effort to find grip for his fingers, he toppled outwards and plunged head downwards over the cliff. Long before the command "hold" could be given we saw him, heels uppermost, arms outspread, knapsack hanging by one strap, and hat rolling into space, on a sloping ice-glazed rock some fifteen feet below us. Burgener, with admirable readiness, had caught hold of the rope as Andenmatten was in the very act of falling, and his iron grip, luckily for us, had stood the strain. I was still clinging to a projecting crag, whilst our last man had thrown himself half over the opposite side of the ridge, and was ready for all emergencies. The fall being checked, all hands seized the rope, but no immediate results ensued. My husband then climbed down, and found that Andenmatten's coat had hitched on a rock. This being loosened, a few strong tugs hauled the victim on to the ridge. The deathly silence was broken only by the sobs of the nerve-shattered bundle which lay at our feet, and it was difficult to realise that this was the same active, sturdy, high-spirited man who had piped for us to dance—who had kept us merry by yodels, making the echoes resound amongst the rocks, and whose cheerfulness had made even the stony moraine and endless screes lose something of their horror. Still the silence remained unbroken save for the injured one's sobs—when, suddenly, a solemn voice remarked, "How providential both bottles of Bouvier are not broken." And, looking round, I found my husband had employed the awe-stricken moments in overhauling the contents of the knapsack. One of these same bottles was promptly opened, and a glass of the foaming fluid poured down the throat of the gasping guide.

After again displaying my great surgical skill, mainly by banging the injured one in the ribs, bending his limbs, and generally treating him in a reckless and unmerciful manner, I declared him more frightened than hurt. "Vörwarts," shouted Burgener; "Vöwarts, wir wollen nicht zurück" [we won't turn back], and once more he took the lead. I followed, then my husband and last of all Andenmatten, his face deathly pale, his limbs trembling, and his head enveloped in a voluminous red handkerchief. At every small rock that came in our way he uttered either bitter curses on the past or prayers for his future; matters, we assured him, of trivial import so long as he placed his feet firmly. A short distance further we were forced off the arête on to the Weingarten face. Every ledge and shelf was here so piled with loose, rolling *débris*, that it was impossible to move without upsetting great slabs and stone. They slid from under our feet, collecting perfect avalanches, as they bounded from ledge to ledge, before taking the last tremendous plunge to the glacier. Coming to the end of these shelves and ledges, we were pulled up by "Blatten" [flakes, apparently referring to the slate-like rocks] and forced to ascend to the ridge once more. By this time the mournful appeals of the crestfallen Andenmatten enlisted our sympathies; and we halted a few minutes to once more examine his back and apply a certain well-known remedy to his lips. At the same time a gentle hint was given that it was quite useless to develop pains of any sort, either in the back or elsewhere, until a more favourable spot should present itself for their treatment.

Putting on the rope once more, the great man of the party [Burgener] advanced to the assault. With great care he got his hands well fixed in a crevice, but above and on either side, as far as he could reach, everything he touched came away, covering me with showers of crumbling shale. I jammed my head against the cliff, but this gave scanty shelter from the sharp-edged, slate-like chips that came flying by, and by the time the order "Come on" was sounded, my fingers and arms were a good deal the worse for wear, and my eyes were full of anything and everything small enough to get into them. But the worst was now to come; how was I to get up without at least slaying those behind me, or, which seemed much more likely, upsetting the whole unstable veneer that covered the face of the cliff? Whenever one stone gave way, those above it came sweeping down in a perfect avalanche, so exciting Burgener's fears that he kept shrieking, "You kill your man if you not more careful are." My own impression was that I should not merely "kill my man," but that the whole party and most of the mountain would be hurled to the glacier beneath. It was, therefore, with a most joyful heart that I at length found myself seated securely on a rock overlooking the snow slope on the left of the arête, and could watch in comfort the miseries of my companions below.

So soon as we had thoroughly realized that no serious injury had been done either to us or the mountain, Burgener carefully examined our route. In a few moments forth came the joyful words, "Herr Mommerie, das geht."

Looking back, the crag we had just left was weird in the extreme; though at the top it was twenty feet or more in breadth, it narrowed down at the bottom of the cleft to less than two feet, and the whole mass looked as if a good blow from an ice-axe would send it bodily on to the Weingarten glacier. Indeed, as the mist whirled and eddied through the cleft, it seemed to totter as in the very act of falling. But it was already 4 P.M., and we were far from the wished for snow; so, whilst Andenmatten was being coached across, my husband unroped and went to work, crawling up a steep "step" in the arête. The rope was then thrown up to him, and Alexander, scrambling up by its aid, was ready to help the rest of the party. This procedure was then repeated. Still crag followed crag, here loose rocks that rolled away at a touch, there precipitous buttresses, access to which could only be gained by using Burgener's broad shoulders as a ladder. All at once, however, difficulties seemed to cease, our leader again put on the rope, and we rattled along the arête till it broadened out into a great snow ridge.

"Der Teufelsgrat ist gemacht!" [has met its match], shouted Burgener, and we began to race along the snow, which rose in front and to our right into a steep crest. Up these slopes we could see the footprints left by a party which, under the leadership of Franz Burgener, had made the ordinary ascent on the previous day. "Half an hour more and it is done, and the Teufelsgrat is ours," added the excited Alexander as we hurried along, feeling that success was within our grasp. The footprints grew perceptibly larger, and on we ran till we actually placed our feet in the tracks. Here all unnecessary luggage was deposited, and Burgener, seeing I was very cold, arrayed me in his coat and gloves. We hastened up the snow, finding no difficulty other than its extreme softness. A scramble over some sharp slate-like rocks followed, then a little more snow, and at 5.30 P.M. we stood on the summit. But for one moment only. At once Burgener began with serious face to say, "I not like a thunderstorm on this ridge." There was no doubt about it, the clouds were wrapping round us, and the distant grumble rolled in our ears. "Go on, go on quicker, Herr Mommerie!" and then with a push he hustled me along the arête. "You must go on, I could a cow hold here," were the encouraging words I heard as I went helter-skelter over anything which happened to be in the way. Soon the snow slopes were reached, and our property once more picked up. We ran our hardest through the blinding storm, almost deafened by the reverberating peals of thunder; but what mattered it? True it was late; true we were cold, hungry, and tired; true we were sinking into the snow above our knees, and the "trace" had disappeared beneath the rapidly falling snow; but "the Teufelsgrat was ours," and we cared little for these minor evils, and we laughed the tempest to scorn with yodels and triumphant shouts. A short traverse to the left and we crossed the Bergschrund; a weary drag over gentle snow slopes, a little care in winding through some open crevasses, and our dangers were ended. At 8 P.M. we reached the snout of the Kien glacier, and once more stepped on to moraine. We descended stony slopes for another hour, and then I remembered that our last meal had taken place at 10 A.M. It being obvious that we could not get to Randa that night, I suggested a halt, and the idea was received with applause. In a few minutes we were sitting on various stones munching our evening meal, the only draw-back being that we were distinctly cold. My hands and feet were numb, and what remained of our clothing (we had left a good deal of it on the Teufelsgrat) was soaking wet, and, worst of all, my boots, viewed by the flickering light of a candle, seemed hardly likely to hold out till we got to Randa.

Our hunger being somewhat appeased, I noticed symptoms of sleepiness amongst the guides. In consequence, I reminded Burgener of his promise to take us, in any case, down to the trees, so that we might rejoice in a fire. We started off once more, carefully roped. The slope being steep and intersected by low cliffs, and the night being so inky black that we could see nothing, it was really necessary to take this precaution. We proceeded down the hill much as a pack of cards might be expected to do. Burgener sprawling on his back and upsetting me, and I passing the shock back to the others. This mode of advance kept up till 11 P.M., when our guides suddenly pulled up, and inquired, in an awestruck whisper, whether we could see a tiny light on the right? With great glee I said, "Yes, it must be a châlet." The suggestion was treated with silent contempt. "What can it be then?" In funereal tones Burgener said, "I do not know;" but Andenmatten timidly whispered, "Geister!" From that moment I could see there was no fire for us; that we should be lucky if we could sneak under the cover of a rock to shelter us from the storm that threatened once more to burst over our heads.

A few steps further and a huge black object faced us. On examination we found it to be a suitable place for spending the next few hours. In five minutes the guides were snoring peacefully; but we, after wringing the water out of our dripping clothes, were reduced to dancing various war dances in the vain hope of keeping warm. When these exercises became unduly fatiguing, we watched the lightning play round the peaks and ridges, and finally stirred up the guides with an ice-axe and urged them to continue the descent. They did not at all approve this course of action, as they considered their quarters luxurious and most thoroughly calculated to induce refreshing sleep. The next two hours were spent in slowly slipping and tumbling down stony grass-grown slopes. We then turned to the right on to somewhat smoother ground. The men, however, refused to go further, alleging that there were fearful precipices in front, and that, in the blackness of the stormy night, it was quite impossible to do so with reasonable safety. The guides again went soundly to sleep, whilst we watched wearily for the first sign of morning. When a streak of light did at length illumine the darkness, we saw the dim outline of trees not far distant, and promptly went down to them. A fire was soon blazing, and we endeavoured to warm ourselves; but though we well nigh roasted our toes and fingers and scorched our faces, the rest of us seemed, perhaps by contrast, colder than before, and we shivered painfully before the crackling pine wood.

As soon as it was fairly light, we dragged our weary bodies through the forest and along and down the pastures, till at 5.30 A.M. we entered the little white inn at Randa. We woke the landlord, and he promptly provided us with a big fire. A hot breakfast followed, and when we had done due justice to his culinary efforts, we climbed into a shaky char-à-banc and drove back to Zermatt.

Burgener was in the highest spirits; his chief source of delight appeared to be a belief that our non-return the previous night would have excited alarm, and that we should probably have the proud privilege of meeting a search party, properly equipped for the transport of our shattered remains. My husband, however, did not altogether sympathise with these feelings, and seemed to have a keen appreciation of the Trinkgeld, tariffs, and other pecuniary concomitants of such luxuries. Happily, we knew our friends were not very likely to think we should have come to any harm, and when two hours later we drove into Zermatt, we found they were still peacefully slumbering in their rooms.

«Watching the spider»

Mrs. E. P. Jackson
and the First Winter Traverse of the Jungfrau, 1888

Mrs. E. P. Jackson was not as well known as such contemporaries as Lucy Walker and Elizabeth Le Blond, but Le Blond herself called her "one of the greatest women climbers of her time." In 1876, she and her husband made a first ascent of the Wiessmies; ten years later, for reasons not entirely clear, she suddenly began ticking off one after another of the great Alpine climbs of the age: the Grand Dru, the Dent Blanche, the Grand Charmoz, and several others.

Until 1887, Jackson climbed only during the summer, but after that she became intrigued with the challenges of winter mountaineering, a fascination that culminated in the winter traverse of the 13,669-foot Jungfrau. A complicated and severe undertaking even in the summer, the Jungfrau crossing had been considered virtually impossible in the winter, and, as Jackson was well aware, had never been accomplished before by climbers of either sex. The editors of the *Alpine Journal* were impressed enough with Jackson's feat that they not only asked her for an account of it, but published it under her name (a courtesy that had been denied Meta Brevoort eighteen years earlier). Jackson seems to have considered this interesting enough to allude to it, albeit subtly, in the opening of her story—where the strange "fate" that awaits her is not the Jungfrau crossing itself, but the *Journal*'s asking her to write about it.

Jackson was apparently a woman of some reserve. At the end of the story below—which appeared in the 1889 *Alpine*

Mr. and Mrs. E. P. Jackson. Studio portrait made in London, possibly 1870s. Courtesy of the Alpine Club Library.

Journal as "A Winter Quartette"—she writes that the "one little cloud" hanging over her Jungfrau traverse was the death, some months later, of one of her guides, Emil Boss—neglecting to mention that following the climb she had lost several of her toes to frostbite and would never be able to climb at such a high standard again.

EITHER THE DAYS of witchcraft are at an end or I am a very degenerate descendant of the once powerful Lancashire witches. No ancestress of mine, taking her midnight ride, ever came to warn me of the fate the weird sisters were perhaps then weaving for me—that one day the story of my winter wanderings in the Alps might be required of me. A most imperfect story too, for I have not a note to go by, since, according to my usual custom, I contrived to lose my pencil—a piece of carelessness, by the way, which, taken with a few other small arrangements of the like nature, often increases the pleasure of the climb. When I started for Grindelwald the Christmas before last it was with the intention of trying what mountain work in the winter was like, and the programme was, if possible, to be brought to a brilliant conclusion by the crossing of the Jungfrau. My husband and I had tried it in bygone years more than once from the Wengern Alp, but without success, and I now thought it was just possible that, with the winter snow, and by starting from the Bergli instead of the Guggi hut, some of the difficulties often met with during the ascent in the summer might be lessened, if not altogether avoided.

On January 10 we were again *en route viâ* the Zäsenberghorn and Viescher glacier for one, perhaps two nights, at the Bergli hut, with the deepest laid schemes concerning the Jungfrau. We found the snow everywhere good, and the crevasses, although large, few in number; but on some of the steeper slopes and at one or two awkward corners steps had to be cut; the porters, too, took their own good time, consequently it was late when we arrived there.

Our good intentions made overnight for an early start up the Jungfrau came, as such things sometimes do, to an untimely end. We overslept ourselves, and by the time we were ready to move had resolved upon a shorter day—either the Mönch or the Gross Viescherhorn. We quickly decided in favour of the latter, for we knew it had never yet been ascended in the winter. With carefully made steps for future use we crossed the lower Mönch Joch to the Ewigschneefeld, and then in truth a surprise and pleasure was waiting for us: it was as hard and firm as any well-laid floor! There was no longer any occasion for those muttered remarks so common to the place, the full meaning of which it is better perhaps not to inquire into too closely, nor for that utter silence telling so plainly the thoughts then passing through one's mind. No, it was a dream of beauty and delight.

We went cheerily along until we were well in front of our peak; then, turning to the left, ascended some long but very easy glacier slopes, made a short halt for our second breakfast, and, crossing the very small bergschrund to a short slope of snow, reached the foot of the rocks a little to the left of the S.S.W. arête by which the remainder of the ascent was made. These rocks were somewhat steep, hidden in part by snow and in one or two places made a little awkward by a glaze of ice, the first we had met with, but it was only enough to suggest some extra care, and without any real difficulty we followed them until we turned on to the actual edge of the arête about a quarter of an hour below the summit.

We stayed there a long time, far too long, indeed, for any chance of reaching the Bergli hut again by daylight, but it was a scene not to be forgotten. . . .

On January 12 we were up early; no more oversleeping, for there was some housemaid's work to be done before closing the door, as we hoped, for the last time. Then retracing our steps by the cheerful light of a lantern as far as the Lower Mönch Joch, we turned to the right and were over the ridge running between the Mönch and Trugberg before the day had shown much sign of breaking. We went along the glacier close by the foot of the Jungfrau Joch, with the Kranzberg well away to the left, and made for the hollow between it and the Jungfrau. The sun had by this time risen, but it was very cold, and we were not at all sorry to begin the ascent of the steep snow slope directly under the well-known bergschrund and Rothtal Sattel. But the higher we went the lower sank our hopes of success. Some time before we had noticed that the Mönch was indulging in a morning pipe, but that we tried to persuade ourselves was only due to some local current. Now, however, there was a most persistent roar among the rocks on our right hand. Was the said local current making itself at home there, or did it extend higher up? We would soon find out, and find out soon we did. We had gone quickly up the slope, for hardly any step-cutting was required, and it was still very cold. We had also made a great pretence of difficulty in crossing the diminished bergschrund, but it was only when we reached the Sattel that we met our cruel enemy face to face. It was blowing half a gale, blowing, it seemed to us, from every quarter at once, and it was only by crouching down on the snow at every blast that we managed to cross the Sattel and ascend even part of the way up the short slope leading towards the lowest ridge of rock overlooking the Rothtal. Thirty, perhaps thirty-five, steps alone separated us from it, and there were distinct marks of old ones the whole way across, but they would have to be cut out again in the hard ice, and in the very teeth of the gale. Almer set to work at once and succeeded in clearing three or four of them, then Christian Jössi, our second guide took his turn, then Mr. Boss, and for nearly three hours they fought desperately against the icy wind without getting even half way to the rocks. They gave in at last, but most unwillingly, and we turned back. Oh the bitter disappointment! We could see that the rocks were perfectly free from snow; the flagstaff on the top, too, was plainly visible in the sunshine, and a very short time would have taken us there if only the wind would have lulled a little. Of course it was then too late in the day to think of crossing, but from the summit we could have seen something of what the north face was like, and that was almost half the work.

We were all half frozen, and our clothes as stiff as boards, so when we got down again to the bergschrund Mr. Boss suggested that it was about time for tea. So leading the way to a small ice cave under the rocky spur running down from the Rothtalhorn, and producing from some mysterious pocket, first some small pieces of wood and then a kettle with a tin cup, he proceeded to make a cheerful little fire in a hole in the ice, and very soon some melted snow was boiling over it. Was ever afternoon tea made in such a place before? We drank it quickly, and after one more long look at the now distant flagstaff started downwards. The steps on the steep slope held well, and before very long we were again on the glacier, making for the Ober Mönch Joch as fast as the now rather soft snow would let us. Darkness fell as we crossed it; we lighted the lanterns; and in due time the four hungry, tired, and much disappointed mortals were back in the Bergli hut. Next morning we returned to Grindelwald, and it was certainly a black moment in my life when I was asked how we had fared, and had to answer that we had failed.

I could not rest; the disappointment on the Jungfrau was for ever in my mind, and with it the old tale of Robert the Bruce watching the spider make its seventh attempt to scale the cottage wall. I thought, too, of the many failures on the Matterhorn and the Aiguille du Dru before either of them was conquered. All this could have but one result. I resolved to try again.

The night of January 15 found us in our old quarters at the Bergli hut, with everything prepared for a good start the next morning. All promised well. It was very cold, but there was no wind; our old steps too served us again, and before very long we were up the steep snow and across the bergschrund on to the Rothtal Shattel, with only the now easy ice-slope between us and the much-wished-for ridge of rock. Here we halted for our second breakfast, with some more wonderful cooking arrangements, and in a short space of time a hot beef steak was handed round, with tea to follow; so, fortified for the work that was before us, we went up the very easy rocks, then the last snow-slope (often a mere knife-edge in summer), and we soon stood on the top—a solid cone of ice. The view, as everyone knows, is lovely; it was on this day clear at all points but the north. We only allowed ourselves, however, a few minutes to admire it, and then, after exchanging friendly greetings with that most modest and retiring peak, the Dent d'Hérens, we commenced the much-longed-for descent.

We were soon down the rocks and ice-slope on to the large snow-field at their base, being helped in part by some old steps which only needed clearing out, and then we went along almost at a run, for we were anxious to save all the time we could. There was not the smallest difficulty; the few crevasses that were open showed no disposition to deceive whatsoever, and were quickly turned either to the right or left as the case might be. It was only on the last slope before reaching the rock arête leading to the Silberlücke that the axe was at all needed. Here, again, was a whole staircase of old steps, a souvenir of the past summer, and, while some of them were being merely cleared out and others entirely recut, it flashed across my mind that the original master hand had been that of Ambrose Supersaxo.

The arête when free from snow must be a perfect walk, not excepting the two last towers above the gap. We had to take it with perhaps a little extra care, devoting our energies to the often vain attempt of keeping either one or both feet out of some wily and unseen trap; but it was a change from the perpetual snow-fields, and did not delay us very much. We made a short halt in the Silberlücke (where a little ladder was quietly enjoying its winter's rest), partly for some half-frozen food, partly to look into the desolate Roththal; then, with a little more help from the axe of the long-departed Supersaxo, and an easy jump over the bergschrund, now shrunk to a mere nothing, we were on the Giessen glacier, running a mild steeplechase over its almost unbroken surface in the direction of the Schneehorn.

At the much-crevassed and broken part, near the Klein Silberhorn, we pulled up. We had no idea as to whether we should have any trouble in passing through it or not. Fortune, however, still favoured us; caution only was necessary, and soon again we were urging our wild career.

It was needful; the light was beginning to fade, and we had still before us the descent of a steep face of rock, with the way afterwards to find through the great ice-fall on to the Guggi glacier. The cornice, too, on the Schneehorn might give us trouble (it did somewhat) and it took some time in the failing light to find a safe place where it could be cut through on to the face of snow between it and the rocks beneath.

Oh! the weary descent of those rocks; they were not only very steep and very rotten, but were much covered with snow in the worst possible condition, and the utmost care was needed to prevent a slip. To make matters even worse, it was by this time quite dark, one of our lanterns obstinately refused to keep lighted, and our only remaining hope had to be continually passed from hand to hand to enable the one person then moving to see where the next step might be.

We were all glad to reach the plateau on which the routes from the Jungfrau and the Jungfrau Joch join, but were getting very anxious about our chance of passing through the ice-fall in the darkness. One lantern can only light up a short distance in front, and the only other thing we had to depend on was a large torch, used, I think, for signalling; this would burn brilliantly, it is true, but for just one half-hour. How we searched for that outlet! first about the middle, then a little to the left, and back again to the centre, then on to the right, but without any success. Another long reconnaissance to the left, then a still longer one, as far as the light of the torch would take us, to the right, but it was of no avail. Finally, returning to the spot we had first started from, Mr. Boss led the way through an arched entrance, and down an inclined plane, into an ice cavern, below the level of the glacier, and said that we must now wait for daylight. It was not exactly the most cheerful prospect, for we were tired and hungry. Our larder, too, was scantily furnished; a very little bread, a small piece of cheese, a few raisins, and a little brandy was all we had—wait, I think I remember seeing also a chicken bone. We could keep ourselves warm though—the cave itself did not feel very cold, and we had with us a large opossum rug, with some other warm garments, so things might have been worse. The cavern was very beautiful; it was divided into two long and narrow chambers by ice pillars, which gradually closed at the far end into a wall; icicles of all shapes and sizes hung from the roof and sides, and the whole place glistened in the light of our faithful lantern. We dug a hole in the snow, carpeting it with empty rucksacks, and using our axes as seats. We dined sumptuously on cheese and raisins (leaving the bread for breakfast); then, putting on every available warm wrap, prepared to get through the night as pleasantly as we could and to make the best of a bad bargain.

Five minutes in the daylight next morning was quite enough to find the long-sought-for chimney—it was hardly twenty paces from where we had spent the night—I think we had been actually on it, but it was so narrow and so much covered by a projecting headland of ice that it was small wonder we had missed it in the darkness. We went down it one by one on to the *débris* of some recently fallen séracs, through which we hurried, meeting on the way two of our old guides, who had come up from Grindelwald the previous afternoon to give us extra help, if necessary, and who, not being able to find the upward path, had spent a much more uncomfortable night than ours in prowling round and round some large blocks of ice.

In a short time we were over the Guggi glacier, all the difficulties behind our backs, and with nothing between us and the Wengern Alp but the tail of the Eiger glacier, its moraine, and the well-known grass slopes beyond, all thickly covered with snow. It is needless to say that we did not linger.

This, my most lame and imperfect tale of our winter wanderings in the High Alps, is now finished, finished too on the anniversary of our first start. How vividly it has brought the whole scene again before me! It was a new experience, but to me a most enjoyable one. All the disagreeables seemed to be in the first 10,000 feet, and from the same cause—deep, powdery snow; higher up they vanished. The cold too was sometimes very severe, especially so directly after sundown, but the pleasant and just sufficient warmth of the sun was most delightful, and when combined as it generally was with firm rocks and good hard snow more than compensated us for any of our earlier troubles. Perhaps we had exceptionally fine and settled weather, I cannot tell. This, however, I do know, that there is just one little cloud to dim the brightness of it all—the thought that never again in any of my future wanderings will I meet the man, who by his great experience in winter climbing, and his unceasing efforts to make all things easy for me, contributed so much to all our success. I mean Mr. Emil Boss.

«A real snorker»

Lily Bristow
Climbs the Grépon, the Dru, and the Rothorn, 1893

Lily Bristow was a skilled rock climber who made several notable ascents with the renowned A. F. Mummery in the 1890s.
It was her 1893 ascent of the Grépon for which she was best
known, but also important in the history of women's climbing
is the fact that Bristow sometimes climbed at the head of the
rope, even on teams that included such well-known climbers
as Mummery, Norman Collie, and Ellis Carr. (The climbs
described below are also notable for having been done without
the assistance of native guides.)

Bristow's Grépon ascent apparently prompted Mummery to
make his notorious remark that "all mountains pass through
three stages—An inaccessible peak—The hardest climb in the
Alps—An easy day for a lady." Although this quip went on to
become a sort of *summa* for mountaineering chauvinists, Bristow
clearly was a better rock climber than many of the men with
whom she climbed, with Mummery noting at one point that her
fluid style on the Grépon "showed the representatives of the
Alpine Club how steep rocks should be climbed." The excerpts
below, from letters written by Bristow to her family and published in 1942 by the *Alpine Journal*, certainly bear out that
assessment, and also provide glimpses of a tough and energetic
personality.

Montenvers,
6th August, 1893.

REJOICE WITH ME, for I have done my peak! the biggest climb I have ever had or ever shall have, for there isn't one to beat it in the Alps (unless it's the traverse of the Meije, which they haven't done yet, but which Fred [Mummery] doesn't believe is as good). Which you mayn't know it, but the expedition I'm referring to is the traverse of the Grépon. On the 3rd, Fred, Mr. Hastings and I tracked off from here, and camped at the same place on the Nantillons Glacier where Fred and I camped before, and where we were driven back by bad weather (*n.b.* I thought that night that three people in one tent 6 ft. × 4 ft. was a tightish fit; but await the sequel). Next morning Mr. Slingsby, Dr. Collie and Mr. Brodie joined us at the camp, having walked from Montenvers about 4.30 A.M., and soon afterwards Fred and I started so as to get the step-cutting done ready for the others when they had breakfasted. After about 1-1/2 hours' going the others caught us up, they only having to walk in our steps, and Mr. Slingsby tied on to our rope, as we three were to go up the Grépon by the couloir and Fred's crack, and the other three were to cross the glacier to C.P. (a rock so called, I don't know why) and work up by Morse and Wicks' route—their route was easier than ours provided they could surmount one very difficult obstacle, which Morse and Wicks had circumvented by rope-throwing. The two parties were to meet on the top, and we were each to descend by the route opposite to that by which we had come. We found our couloir, however, not in the very best imaginable condition, even at that early hour of the morning, so Fred and Mr. Slingsby immediately decided that the other party must be persuaded to return with us by the C.P. route. Well, it's no good trying to describe the climb; I have often felt, on the climbs, that if I had sufficient knowledge and pluck I could have done it by myself, but this climb was something totally different. It was more difficult than I could ever imagine—a succession of problems, each one of which was a ripping good climb in itself—you will understand well enough that in a climb of this kind there is not the slightest danger for any one except the leading man, the others merely follow in absolute safety with the rope, but certainly with vast exertion. Fred is magnificent, he has such absolute confidence, I never once had the faintest squirm about him even when he was in the most hideous places, where the least slip would have been certain death, and there were very many such situations. It is really a huge score for him to have taken me (*and* the camera) on such an expedition. I took six photographs, and have developed two, one of which is a failure. Well, we got to the top but saw no signs of the other party—we yodelled, yelled and howled but heard no reply and Mr. Slingsby began to be seriously alarmed for their safety. However, we proceeded on our way, along a series of summits (for the Grépon has even more peaks than the Charmoz, which as you know has five). When we got to the final peak, our shouts were at last answered from below, the other party having been stopped by the obstacle I mentioned, where Morse and Wicks threw ropes. As Dr. Collie and Mr. Hastings had been up before, and as it was getting late in the afternoon (about 4.30) they remained where they were, while Fred and Mr. Slingsby hauled up Mr. Brodie with two ropes. Then we all descended to the other two, who had got some tea and bread and butter and other luxuries ready for us—then I took some more photographs, and as the situation did not admit of setting up a tripod Mr. Hastings made a support for me by wedging his head against a rock. By this time it was beginning to get dark and also heavy mists came up, which soon turned to rain. As I had been delayed by the photography, one party (Dr. Collie and Messrs. Slingsby and Brodie) went on, and the rest of us followed as soon as possible. Our party went on ahead, as it was rapidly getting dark and raining hard, while Mr. Slingsby's remarks drifted to us through the pauses in the wind. At last we failed to find the tracks by which the other party had ascended in the morning, so Dr. Collie's party who had a lantern, went ahead, and Dr. C. who is a marvellous pathfinder succeeded after about an hour in recovering the track. Everybody was wet through except myself, who was only partially so, as I was wearing Fred's short waterproof coat. We reached our camp soon after 11 P.M. and *now* is the sequel I mentioned. Imagine six people in a tent which had been tight for three! Sleeping-bags, tent and every-thing were of course sopping wet, but it was bliss and comfort after our experiences outside. Fred pulled off my boots and wormed me into a wet sleeping-bag, and I lay down in the shallowest part of the pool and felt heavenly comfortable and warm. The other poor devils all had to sit up, as there was no room for them to lie down, and they must have been horribly cold and wet. I actually went to sleep for a short time. We all of us got cramp more or less, and that ain't pleasant, when it is absolutely impossible to move. The wind was that rampageous, that I can't imagine how the fellows managed to hold the tent down at all. As soon as it was light enough we crawled down the wet slippery rocks, and traversed the bergschrund below, and I suppose we got to Montenvers about 8 A.M. faint yet pursuing. That was yesterday. I promptly went to bed after some hot milk and came to lunch with a gorgeous appetite, a very good temper, extremely sore hands, and a general feeling of gratified ambition. I am perfectly fit today, and Mares [Mary Mummery] and I are going to track round with the fellows to their *gîte* [cottage] from which place they are going to make another attempt on the Aiguille du Plan.

> Montenvers,
> 10th August, 1893.

The day before yesterday we camped out for the Dru, as we have been having such perfect weather that it seemed wicked not to use our opportunities, although the gentlemen were all rather tired from their ascent of the Plan—Fred, Mr. Slingsby and I had the tent, and Dr. Collie and Mr. Hastings camped under a rock, and all passed a most comfortable night. I am getting quite swagger at sleeping on stones. As for my ankle, thanks, it is almost as good as new again. I can now walk all right on a path or a glacier; and on loose stones, one or other of the gentlemen always gives me a hand. We left our camp for the Dru about 3 A.M., it was no good starting earlier, as all the ground was fairly difficult, so it was necessary to be able to see one's way. First we went over a stretch of glacier, and then took to the rocks—Fred and I on one rope, and the other fellows together—we had none of us ever been up before, but I had been fortunate enough to spot a party coming down from the col with guides the previous evening, and had very carefully noted their route, so I had some idea of the way; this being so, Fred let me lead, which I always enjoy, it is so much more exciting. We reached the col about half-past five, and breakfasted there; we had had some tea before leaving the camp. By this time we had come to much more difficult rocks, and though we remained in the same order for about half an hour, it soon became necessary for us all to go on one rope, as no one but Fred could lead up some of the places, and even he only with Mr. Hastings to give him a shoulder up, so he, Mr. H., came second on the rope, then I, and then Mr. Slingsby, and Dr. Collie last. The climbing was pretty stiff, I must say, though not nearly so difficult as the Grépon, which is a real snorker. When we got to the top I was a good deal tired, so Fred put me in a safe place and I had a snooze, and when I woke the fellows gave me a lovely drink of lemons and half-melted snow. By this time I suppose it was about twelve. Going down we took a great deal longer than we ought to have done, but we were all tired; however, we got back to the camp just before dark. Dr. Collie and Mr. Hastings had gone on ahead and had made me some tea, which revived me sufficiently for the rest of the journey. We had now some rather slabby sort of rocks to go down, and the only way we could find was along the track of a small waterfall, so we got drenched to the skin—however, in about half an hour we were down the slabs, and then we had interminable moraine. I should have been quite dead, only Mr. Hastings, the Hercules of the party, gave me a hand all the way, and got me along so quickly that we managed to reach the hotel by 11.30, and very glad of our victuals we were when we got them. We all feel as though we deserved some rest, so we are lazing, and talk of leaving here tomorrow for the Chalet de Lognan, a sort of little mountain pub, where there are said to be three beds—I suppose the others will camp on the floor somewhere. After a couple of days there, at the outside, I expect we shall go on to Zinal; where my address will be Hotel Durand—after that we shall be at Breuil on the Italian side, and shall eventually return here for our baggage. We have just heard of the accident on the Matterhorn, Gentinetta (one of the guides here) has had a postcard from his brother at Zermatt—we get so little news here except what one picks up in that sort of way. There is a rumour too, of an accident on the Grandes Jorasses, but I hope there is no truth in it.

If you only knew how awfully good all those fellows are in taking care of me, you would not feel the least anxiety about my safety or comfort—they all try to see who can do the most coddling, and I am even more cosseted than I used to be when I was alone with Fred. Except a wholesome sort of laziness, I am just as fit as I can be today, and my appetite is large enough to make the chef shudder—I only had my breakfast about 11, but at one o'clock I repaired to lunch with quite unabated vigour. Fred's exploits here are creating a great deal of enthusiasm. His having taken a lady up the two most difficult peaks here, without guides, in the course of one week, and having sandwiched between these expeditions a totally new ascent of a very difficult peak, is really worthy of some applause.

Zinal,
15th August, 1893.

On Monday evening, about 9 o'clock Fred proposed that we should go up the Rothorn next day, so we hastily made preparations and retired to bed. We got up at 1.30, but the natives were so astonished at our enterprise that, though we had ordered our breakfast beforehand, we had to wait countless ages, and only got off at a quarter to three. I had a moke for an hour and a half up the valley, and very glad I was of it, as there was a colossal distance to traverse before we got to the peak at all. About 7 A.M. Fred told me it was quite out of the question that we should get up, that the distance was too great, but I begged and prayed in my most artful manner, and he agreed to go on a bit and see—we made all sorts of little vows—if we didn't get to the col by 10 we would turn back—at 2 o'clock we would turn back, wherever we were—and so on. As a matter of fact we didn't reach the col by ten, but I concealed the fact from Fred, and at last we triumphantly reached the top 25 minutes to two. Then we scrambled down as fast as we could, and if the old fool of a rope didn't go and knock my very superior hat and my goggles down a quite impossible slope and so completely ruin my cherished complexion! I have preserved my skin hitherto with the utmost skill, but of course having no hat has brought my forehead up into the regulation blisters, and even the rest of my face smiles with difficulty. When we got in about 9 P.M. it was a great joke, none of the hotel people would believe we had been up the Rothorn: "non, Mademoiselle, pas possible!" They are not used to non-guided parties here and the idea that Fred and I could calmly track up their most awesome and revered peak is quite beyond them— they think we must have mistaken some grassy knoll for the Rothorn.

«Forty-eight hours on the rope»

Gertrude Bell
Attempts the Northeast Arête of the Finsteraarhorn, 1902

Gertrude Lowthian Bell, born in England in 1868, led a remarkable life both on and off the mountains. Her education at Oxford's Lady Margaret Hall reached a brilliant conclusion when, at the age of twenty, she became the first woman at the university to earn "first class" honors in the field of modern history. Later she traveled and explored widely in the Middle East, writing more than a dozen books about the region. She also became a key administrative figure in the British Empire, serving variously on the Arab Intelligence Bureau in Cairo, as Assistant Political Officer at Basra, and as Oriental Secretary to both the Civil Commissioner of Baghdad and the High Commissioner of Iraq.

Bell did not do any serious climbing until she was thirty years old, but she took to the sport quickly and soon discovered that the hardest climbs brought out the best in her. One of her guides, Ulrich Fuhrer, praised her technical skill, her endurance under extreme conditions, and her cool bravery. One incident in particular reveals this latter quality. During an attempt on the Engelhorn, Ulrich and his brother Heinrich were stymied by a short wall of blank rock. Ulrich, in the lead, tried to get over the impasse by standing on his brother's shoulders in order to reach a secure handhold. When this failed, Bell added herself to the steadily lengthening human ladder:

> Ulrich tried it on Heinrich's shoulder and could not reach any hold.
> I then clambered up onto Heinrich, Ulrich stood on me and fin-

gered up the rock as high as he could. It wasn't high enough. I lifted myself still a little higher—always with Ulrich on me, mind!—and he began to raise himself by his hands. As his foot left my shoulder I put up a hand, straightened out my arm and made a ledge for him. He called out, "I don't feel at all safe—if you move we are all killed." I said, "All right, I can stand here for a week."

Later, when they were all safely past this desperate passage, Ulrich told her that if "when I was standing on your shoulders and asked if you felt safe, you had said you did not, I should have fallen and we should all have gone over." Bell replied: "I thought I was falling when I spoke."

Bell's energetically written account of her attempt on the 14,026-foot Finsteraarhorn—on which she and the Fuhrer brothers were driven back by a storm, spent two shelterless nights out on the peak, and nearly lost their toes to frostbite— is reprinted from a letter to her stepbrother, Hugh, published in 1927 in *The Letters of Gertrude Bell.*

THE MATTER we had in hand was the ascent of the face of the Finsteraarhorn: it is a well-known problem and the opinions of the learned are divided as to its solution. Dr. Wilson looked at it this year and decided against it. We have looked at it for 2 years and decided for it and other authorities agree with us in what I still think is a right opinion.

Thursday. Crossed the séracs just at dawn and by 6 found ourselves comfortably established on the arête, beyond the reach of the stones which the mountain had fired at us (fortunately with rather a bad aim) for the first half-hour on the rock. We breakfasted then followed a difficult and dangerous climb. It was difficult because the rocks were exceedingly steep, every now and then we had to creep up and out of the common hard chimney—one in particular about mid-day, I remember, because we subsequently had the very deuce of a time coming down it, or round the face of a tower or cut our way across an ice couloir between two gendarmes and it was dangerous because the whole rock was so treacherous. I found this out very early in the morning by putting my hand into the crack of a rock which looked as if it went into the very foundation of things. About two feet square of rock tumbled out upon me and knocked me a little way down the hill

till I managed to part company with it on a tiny ledge. I got back on to
my feet without being pulled up by the rope, which was as well for a
little later I happened to pass the rope through my hands and found
that it had been cut half through about a yard from my waist when the
rock had fallen on it. This was rather a nuisance as it shortened a rope
we often wanted long to allow of our going up difficult chimneys in
turn. So on and on we went up the arête and the towers multiplied like
rabbits above and grew steeper and steeper and about 2 o'clock I
looked round and saw great black clouds rolling up from the west. But
by this time looking up we also saw the topmost tower of the arête far
above us still, and the summit of the mountain further still and though
we could not yet see what the top of the arête was like we were cheered
and pushed on steadily for another hour while the weather signs got
worse and worse. At 3 just as the first snow flakes began to fall, we got
into full view of the last two gendarmes—and the first one was quite
impossible. The ridge had been growing narrow, its sides steeper as we
mounted, so that we had been obliged for some time to stick quite to
the backbone of it; then it threw itself up into a great tower leaning
over to the right and made of slabs set like slates on the top with a
steep drop of some 20 feet below them on to the col. We were then
1000 feet below the summit I should guess, perhaps rather less, anyway
we could see our way up, not easy but possible, above this tower and
once on the top we could get down the other side in any weather. It
had to be tried: we sat down to a few mouthfuls the snow falling fast,
driven by a strong wind, and a thick mist marching up the valley
below, over the Finsteraar joch, then we crept along the knife edge of a
col, fastened a rope firmly round a rock and let Ulrich down on to a
ledge below the overhang of the tower. He tried it for a few moments
and then gave it up. The ledge was very narrow, sloped outward and
was quite rotten. Anything was better than that. So we tried the left
side of the tower: there was a very steep iced couloir running up at the
foot of the rock on that side for about 50 feet, after which all would be
well. Again we let ourselves down on the extra rope to the foot of the
tower, again to find that this way also was impossible. A month later in
the year I believe this couloir would go; after a warm August there
would be no ice in it, and though it is very steep the rocks so far as one
could see under the ice, looked climbable. But even with the alternative before us of the descent down the terrible arête, we decided to
turn back; already the snow was blowing down the couloir in a small
avalanche, small but blinding, and the wind rushed down upon us

carrying the mists with it. If it had been fine weather we should have tried down the arête a little and then a traverse so as to get at the upper rocks by another road. I am not sure that it could be done but we should have tried anything—but by the time we had been going down for half-an-hour we could see nothing of the mountain side to the right or to the left except an occasional glimpse as one cloud rolled off and another rolled over. The snow fell fast and covered the rocks with incredible speed. Difficult as they had been to go up, you may imagine what they were like going down when we could no longer so much as see them.

There was one corner in particular where we had to get round the face of a tower. We came round the corner, down a very steep chimney, got on to a sloping out rock ledge with an inch of new snow on it; there was a crack in which you could stand and with one hand hold in the rock face, from whence you had to drop down about eight feet on to steep snow. We fixed the extra rope and tumbled down one after the other on to the snow; it was really more or less safe because one had the fixed rope to hold on to, but it felt awful: I shall remember every inch of that rock face for the rest of my life. It was now near 6. Our one idea was to get down to the chimney—the mid-day chimney which was so very difficult—so as to do it while there was still only a little snow on it. We toiled on till 8, by which time a furious thunderstorm was raging. We were standing by a great upright on the top of a tower when suddenly it gave a crack and a blue flame sat on it for a second, just like the one we saw when we were driving, you remember, only nearer. My ice axe jumped in my hand and I thought the steel felt hot through my woollen glove—was that possible? I didn't take my glove off to see! Before we knew where we were the rock flashed again—it was a great sticking out stone and I expect it attracted the lightning, but we didn't stop to consider this theory but tumbled down a chimney as hard as ever we could, one on top of the other, buried our ice axe heads in some shale at the bottom of it and hurriedly retreated from them. It's not nice to carry a private lightning conductor in your hand in the thick of a thunderstorm. It was clear we could go no further that night, the question was to find the best lodging while there was still light enough to see. We hit upon a tiny crack sheltered from the wind, even the snow did not fall into it. There was just room for me to sit in the extreme back of it on a very pointed bit of rock; by doubling up I could even get my head into it. Ulrich sat on my feet to keep them warm and Heinrich just below him. They each of them put their feet

into a knapsack which is the golden rule of bivouac. The other golden
rule is to take no brandy because you feel the reaction more after. I
knew this and insisted on it. It was really not so bad; we shivered all
night but our hands and feet were warm and climbers are like Pobbles
in the matter of toes. I went to sleep quite often and was wakened up
every hour or so by the intolerable discomfort of my position, which I
then changed by an inch or two into another which was bearable for
an hour more. At first the thunderstorm made things rather exciting.
The claps followed the flashes so close that there seemed no interval
between them. We tied ourselves firmly on to the rock above lest as
Ulrich philosophically said one of us should be struck and fall out. The
rocks were all crackling round us and fizzing like damp wood which is
just beginning to burn—have you ever heard that? It's a curious exciting sound rather exhilarating—and as there was no further precaution
possible I enjoyed the extraordinary magnificence of the storm with a
free mind: it was worth seeing. Gradually the night cleared and became beautifully starry. Between 2 and 3 the moon rose, a tiny crescent, and we spoke of the joy it would be when the sun rose full on to
us and stopped our shivering. But the sun never rose at all—at least for
all practical purposes. The day came wrapped in a blinding mist and
heralded by a cutting, snow-laden wind—this day was Friday; we never
saw the sun in it. It must have snowed a good deal during the thunderstorm for when we stepped out of our crack in the first grey light about
4 (too stiff to bear it a moment longer) everything was deep in it. I can
scarcely describe to you what that day was like. We were from 4 A.M. to
8 P.M. on the arête; during that time we ate for a minute or two 3 times
and my fare I know was 5 ginger bread biscuits, 2 sticks of chocolate, a
slice of bread, a scrap of cheese and a handful of raisins. We had
nothing to drink but about two tablespoonfuls of brandy in the bottom
of my flask and a mouthful of wine in the guides' wine skin, but it was
too cold to feel thirsty. There was scarcely a yard which we could come
down without the extra rope; you can imagine the labour of finding a
rock at every fifty feet round which to sling it, then of pulling it down
behind us and slinging it again. We had our bit of good luck—it never
caught all day. But both the ropes were thoroughly iced and terribly
difficult to manage, and the weather was appalling. It snowed all day
sometimes softly as decent snow should fall, sometimes driven by a
furious bitter wind which enveloped us not only in the falling snow,
but lifted all the light powdery snow from the rocks and sent it whirl-
ing down the precipices and into the couloirs and on to us indif-

ferently. It was rather interesting to see the way a mountain behaves in a snowstorm and how avalanches are born and all the wonderful and terrible things that happen in high places. The couloirs were all running with snow rivers—we had to cross one and a nasty uncomfortable process it was. As soon as you cut a step it was filled up before you could put your foot into it. But I think that when things are as bad as ever they can be you cease to mind them much. You set your teeth and battle with the fates; we meant to get down whatever happened and it was such an exciting business that we had no time to think of the discomfort. I know I never thought of the danger except once and then quite calmly. I'll tell you about that presently. The first thing we had to tackle was the chimney. We had to fix our rope in it twice, the second time round a very unsafe nail [i.e., piton]. I stood in this place holding Heinrich, there was an overhang. He climbed a bit of the way and then fell on to soft snow and spun down the couloir till my rope brought him up with a jerk. Then he got up on to a bit of rock on the left about half as high as the overhang. Ulrich came down to me and I repeated Heinrich's maneuver exactly, the iced extra rope slipping through my hands like butter. Then came Ulrich. He was held by Heinrich and me standing a good deal to the left but only half as high up as he. He climbed down to the place we had both fallen from asking our advice at every step, then he called out "Heinrich, Heinrich, ich bin verloren" [I'm lost], and tumbled off just as we had done and we held him up in the couloir, more dead than alive with anxiety. We gave him some of our precious brandy on a piece of sugar and he soon recovered and went on as boldly as before. We thought the worst was over but there was a more dangerous place to come. It was a place that had been pretty difficult to go up, a steep but short slope of iced rock by which we had turned the base of a tower. The slope was now covered with about 4 inches of avalanche snow and the rocks were quite hidden. It was on the edge of a big couloir down which raced a snow river. We managed badly somehow; at any rate, Ulrich and I found ourselves on a place where there was not room for us both to stand, at the end of the extra rope. He was very insecure and could not hold me, Heinrich was below on the edge of the couloir, also very insecure. And here I had to refix the extra rope on a rock a little below me so that it was practically no good to me. But it was the only possible plan. The rock was too difficult for me, the stretches too big, I couldn't reach them: I handed my axe down to Heinrich and told him I could do nothing but fall, but he couldn't, or at any rate, didn't secure himself and in a second we were both tumbling head over heels down the couloir, which was, you understand, as steep as snow could lie. How Ulrich held us I don't know. He said himself he would not have believed it possible but hearing me say I was going to fall he had stuck the pointed end of the ice axe into a crack above and on this alone we all three held. I got on to my feet in the snow directly I came to the end of my leash of rope and held Heinrich and caught his ice axe and mine and we slowly cut ourselves back up the couloir to the foot of the rock. But it was a near thing and I felt rather ashamed of my part in it. This was the time when I thought it on the cards we should not get down alive. Rather a comforting example, however, of how little can hold a party up. About 2 in the afternoon we all began to feel tired. I had a pain through my shoulder and down my back which was due, I think, to nothing but the exertion of rock climbing and the nervous fatigue of shivering—for we never stopped shivering all day, it was impossible to control one's tired muscles in that bitter cold. And so we went on for six hours more of which only the last hour was easy and at 8 found ourselves at the top of the Finsteraar glacier and in the dark, with a good guess and good luck, happened on the right place in the Bergschrund and let ourselves down over it. It was now quite dark, the snow had turned into pouring rain, and we sank six inches into the soft glacier with every step. Moreover we were wet through: we had to cross several big crevasses and get down the sérac before we could reach the Unteraar glacier and safety. For this we had felt no anxiety having relied upon our lantern but not a single match would light. We had every kind with us in metal match boxes but the boxes were wet and we had not a dry rag of any kind to rub them with. We tried to make a tent out of my skirt and to light a match under it, but our fingers were dripping wet and numb with cold—one could scarcely feel anything smaller than an ice axe— and the match heads dropped off limply into the snow without so much as a spark. Then we tried to go on and after a few steps Heinrich fell into a soft place almost up to his neck and Ulrich and I had to pull him out with the greatest difficulty and the mists swept up over the glacier and hid everything; that was the only moment of despair. We had so looked forward to dry blankets in the Pavillon Dollfus and here we were with another night out before us. And a much worse one than the first, for we were on the shelterless glacier and in driving drenching rain. We laid our three axes together and sat on them side by side. Ulrich and I put our feet into a sack but Heinrich refused to use the other and gave it to me to lie on. My shoulders ached and ached. I insisted on our all eating something even the smallest scrap, and then I put a wet pocket-handkerchief over my face to keep the rain from beating on it and went to sleep. It sounds incredible but I think we all slept more or less and woke up to the horrible discomfort and went to sleep again. I consoled myself by thinking of Maurice in S. Africa and how he had slept out in the pouring rain and been none the worse. We couldn't see the time but long before we expected it a sort of grey light came over the snow and when at last I could read my watch, behold it was 4. We gathered ourselves up; at first we could scarcely stand but after a few steps we began to walk quite creditably. About 6 we got to where we could unrope—having been 48 hours on the rope—and we reached here at 10 on Saturday.

They had all been in a great state of anxiety about us, seeing the weather, and had telegraphed to Meiringen, to Grindelwald, to know whether we had turned up. So I got into a warm bath and then discovered to my great surprise that my feet were ice cold and without any sensation. But having eaten a great many boiled eggs and drunk jugs of hot milk I went to bed and woke about dinner time to find my toes swollen and stiff. Frau Lieseguay then appeared and said that a S. American doctor had passed through in the afternoon and had seen Ulrich and Heinrich and had bound up their hands and feet in cotton wool and told them to keep very warm; so she bound up my feet too— my hands are nearly all right but I think my feet are worse than theirs. Still they seem better now and I don't expect I shall be toeless. They are not nearly as bad as my hands were in the Dauphiné, but the worst of it is that with swollen toes bound up in cotton wool one can't walk at all and I shall just have to wait till they get better. I slept for about 24 hours only waking up to eat, and it's now 4 in the afternoon and I'm just going to get up and have tea with Mr. Campbell, who has, I hear, been an angel of kindness to my guides. They seem to be none the worse except that Ulrich had a touch of rheumatism this morning, and as for me, I am perfectly absolutely well except for my toes—not so much as a cold in the head.

«As no map could show them»

Fanny Bullock Workman
Explores the Glaciers of the Karakorum, 1908

Fanny Bullock was born in 1859 into a prominent and wealthy Massachusetts family. She was educated in New England, then in France and Germany. At age twenty-two she married a physician, William Hunter Workman, who was ten years her senior. In 1889 William retired, and a year later the Workmans set out on a series of incredible bicycle tours: first across Europe, later to Algeria and the Atlas Mountains, then across Spain, Ceylon, and India. On the heels of these journeys appeared three travel books—*Algerian Memories, Sketches Awheel in* fin de siècle *Iberia,* and *Through Town and Jungle*—that were notable less for their literary quality than for the unusual partnership they embodied. Each was a collaborative effort, with the title page listing the authors as they always presented themselves in public, not as Mr. and Mrs. Workman but as Fanny Bullock Workman and William Hunter Workman.

The first of the Workmans' Himalayan expeditions, from Kashmir to Ladakh, came in the summer of 1898. This trip was successful, but their subsequent attempt to continue across Sikkim failed when relations broke down with their porters. (For all the avant-garde egalitarianism of their own marriage, the Workmans were retrograde in their relations with native peoples—whom, as is evident in the account below, they often treated with imperialistic contempt.) In 1899 the couple returned to Kashmir, this time with an experienced Swiss guide on their payroll, and proceeded to climb and name a series of

peaks, foremost among them 21,000-foot Koser Gunge. Though
not particularly impressive by Himalayan standards, the latter
was high enough for Workman to claim the women's altitude
record. She was forty years old at the time, and her newly
begun Himalayan climbing career was to continue until she was
fifty-three. She reached her highest elevation in 1906 with an
ascent of 22,810-foot Pinnacle Peak in the Nun Kun Range of
India. She publicly disputed Annie Smith Peck's claim, made
two years earlier, of having climbed higher on Huascarán in the
Andes—proving her point by sponsoring a survey party that triangulated Peck's high point, which turned out to be a thousand
feet lower than Pinnacle Peak.

The contemporary scientific establishment took the Workmans' endeavors quite seriously—though today, with the exception of their truly pioneering Siachen Glacier expedition of
1912, they are less highly regarded—and when they were not
away in the mountains they kept up a busy schedule of lecturing
and writing, producing five Himalayan travel books and several
magazine articles. Workman addressed such groups as the
Alpine Club and the Royal Geographic Society, whose halls
could at times be as chilly to the woman explorer as the glaciers
of the Himalaya. What most offended the patriarchal sensi-
bilities of some of her peers, apparently, was not her overt feminism but her forthright personality and undeniable successes,
and while it was said that her husband "wielded a pretty blade,
never so keen or so quick as in her support," Workman was
clearly quite capable of defending herself, her response to sexism
being to "sustain her opinions by vigorous arguments based on
facts which it was difficult to controvert."

For the chauvinists, perhaps the unkindest cut of all was
the fact that Fanny was the driving force in the Workman partnership. This was no secret; the *Alpine Journal*, following
Fanny's death in 1925, acknowledged that she had been the
mastermind of their most ambitious undertaking, the 1912
Siachen Glacier exploration, and noted tellingly how it was
William who was "always ready to help her carry out her great
journeys," and not the other way around.

The following account of the Workmans' exploration of the
Hispar Glacier was not written collaboratively but by Bullock
Workman herself, and was published in a New York magazine,

Fanny Bullock Workman in camp in the Himalaya. Date unknown (but between 1898 and 1912). Photographer unknown. Courtesy of the Library of Congress.

the *Independent* (whose occasionally idiosyncratic spellings have been retained here). She had earlier read a draft of the essay before the Royal Geographical Society in London, prompting the president of the Society to write that "the feats accomplished by Mrs. Workman are more remarkable in the way of mountaineering than those which have been accomplished ever before by any of her sex. Whether I ought to make that limitation or not I am rather doubtful, but, at all events, with that limitation it will not be denied."

SIX YEARS AGO, with Petigax and Savoye, Italian guides, I made the first ascent of the Alchori Col, 17,000 feet, at the head of the Alchori Glacier, in Baltistan, with the hope of discovering a new snow passage over which our caravan could be taken to the Hispar. But instead of finding a pass descending to that glacier, I found myself perched on a snow cornice overlooking a precipice of 2,000 feet sheer, below which ran the lonely Hispar, a long, crevassed river, encased northward by lofty, unknown, unnamed mountains.

I turned away, balked by the precipice, but the lure of unexplored mountain wastes held me, as it often does, in its grip, and I determined some day to reach at least the feet of the snow giants, between me and which Nature had here placed such a formidable barrier.

Had we been able to cross the Karakoram watershed at this point we should have had the Hispar and its snow treasures, so to speak, well in hand; whereas, when some years later it was reached, there was a weary prelude of 300 miles of nude valleys and high passes to be played before arriving even at its tongue.

Still, most disagreeable things offer compensations, and such were, this time, that we took to the Hispar a thoroly organized caravan, including two topographers, who were to make a detailed glacial survey of it and its large unknown branches, on the plan sometimes carried out in the Alps and America, but not before attempted in the Himalaya.

That such an expedition involved an immense amount of previous organization and continual work and calculation during the time we were on the glaciers may be seen from the fact that the seventy or more coolies employed had to be fed by us, and the grain and rice requisite for this purpose had, much of it, to be brought from Kashmir, 300 miles, and the remainder supplied by the Mir of Nagar, living 30 miles from Hispar village, the last inhabited spot.

The expedition was divided into two parties. The topographers, with camp outfit, native servants, and about ten coolies, carried on the survey as the nature of their work and the weather admitted of doing. Our caravan consisted of Dr. Hunter Workman, myself, Cyprien Savoye, guide, three Italian porters, native headman and coolies. We continued our explorations and observations of glaciers and ascents of cols and peaks independently, meeting the surveyors from time to time to compare notes.

Our own caravan was also often divided for days, the cook, with large tents, bulk of supplies and sheep being left at a base of perhaps 15,000 feet, while, with light tents, guides, porters and a few coolies we explored and climbed for five or six days, until driven back to the base by bad weather. Such were the conditions of our nomad life on the Hispar for eight weeks.

While investigating a branch glacier which enters the Hispar at 15 miles from its tongue, a fine snow mountain attracted our attention, which, if it could be scaled, would offer a capital station for study of the region and a magnificent panorama.

The question was, Could it be climbed? From a projecting snow mamelon on its west shoulder the final thousand feet looked possible enough, but below this mamelon the mountain fell in ice-falls, seamed both longitudinally and horizontally by gaping crevasses, or in snow-scarps of appalling steepness, to near where it took its rise from the glacier. This was only typical of the character of the whole army of peaks surrounding the Hispar.

On other great Asiatic glaciers one sees mountains with at least some moderate, clean-cut slopes, which tempt the climber to try his luck on them, but such is not the case with these forbidding giants. Studying the Hispar system from any eminence, one is permeated with the fanciful impression that a succession of mighty earth vibrations must at some time have shaken the peaks into the chaotic riven slopes, savage rock precipices, and splintered or corniced pinnacles they now present; not rational, normal mountains any longer, but colossi of rock and snow chaos, with scarcely a ledge or cranny where even a mountain demon could lodge with safety.

On this particular ascent the greatest danger was from avalanches, which scored the lower two-thirds of the mountain from noon until after nightfall. With a few coolies we ascended one afternoon to the top of the glacier, and putting up some *tentes d'abries* sent back the coolies to the lower camp with orders to return the next day at noon. Savoye, the guide, strode across the glacier before sunset to examine the mountain and plan a route, as he was very keen on starting by 2 A.M. and we should have to make our path by lantern-light only.

A few hours' rest in the sleep-sacks and Savoye was heard calling a reveil [*sic*] outside the tents. Coffee made on the small kerosene stoves followed as soon as possible, and sharp at 2 o'clock, after crowding coats and provisions for the day into the rück-sacks, we started forth roped in two caravans. The firmament was brilliant with stars but no waning moon lighted the gray, hardly perceptible snow waste.

Progress was rapid for a few minutes over a gently rising plateau, and then the gradient grew apace and with it came a big ice-fall composed of tall pinnacles or séracs, separated by bottomless chasms. Savoye turned sharp to the right hoping to contour them, but here, as far as we could see, rose a terrace of long crevasses ready to receive us into their creepy depths.

"Sapristi," quoth Savoye, "quelle route." But his eagle eye spied a narrow snow band, near the center of the first crevasse, and by stepping gingerly sideways this was passed and a dozen steps upward brought us to the next yawning ice-mouth. This proved less accommodating than the first crevasse and offered no bridge at all. After scanning its fifty or more feet of length with the lantern, the only way over appeared to be a jump near its narrower end.

Paying out the rope the guide bounded over, then drawing it taut and cautioning the porter behind me to look out for his end called, "Sautez, Madame." How I hated that leap in the dark across the four or five feet of invisible space, but it had to be done, so taking the plunge I landed on the ice-slant where the guide stood. The others followed in turn and slowly, sometimes jumping, sometimes bridging and again finding a way around them, we conquered seven or eight enormous chasms.

Then a steep, frozen scarp awaited us, which was manageable by cutting steps up its ice surface. This ended at the foot of a series of tall white cones which, as Savoye held the lantern aloft, loomed above like a bevy of mountain-spectres assembled in ghostly array to warn us to be sensible and return forthwith whence we had come. But we were bound they should receive us, and as they proved to be solid spectres we cut steps up and down several, wound a way round others, and finally got above the whole bad lot and reached a wide bed of avalanche-débris, which had fallen during the warm hours of the previous day.

Here, where after sunrise it would be folly to tarry a moment, we flung ourselves down after two hours' arduous work to breakfast and watch the wonderful spectacle of dawn in the upper snow world. Dawn is beautiful in the plains of India when heralded by the swish and twitter of innumerable song-birds, but a thousand times more exquisite is the approach of day above all camps and abodes of humanity, beyond even the voice of the high-flying mountain-chough, where only the soft whisper of the breeze from virgin summits breathes its music on the ear. Imperceptibly, as we sat among the avalanches, the curtain of darkness which had held us in bondage was raised, and on all sides peaks, ice-falls and glaciers emerged before our gaze in the solemn magnificence of before sunrise lighting.

While we reveled in the glory of the eternal snows, Savoye, tho ardently discussing cold meat and jam, stood with his eyes riveted on the sharp, almost perpendicular 700 foot wall which loomed in mauve toning just beyond the plowed-up snowfield where we halted. Up this great snow-scarf lay, perforce, our route. At one end of it, which luckily we should not touch, hung great stratified ice-cornices shimmering in weird beauty now, but ready later, when the sun burned upon them, to fall in deadly ice-masses to enhance the tumbled hillocks of snow-débris we were about to leave.

The ropes being adjusted again in fifteen minutes its base was reached where constant step-cutting and serious climbing was in order for over an hour.

Here we climbed straight, there we zig-zagged, as snow conditions demanded, making steady headway, the surface remaining hard even after the first sun's rays fell upon it. It was severe and ticklish traveling and each man had to look out that he did not slither and plunge his caravan down the precipice to a useless end among the fallen avalanches.

Two or three times, when it was possible to halt a bit, the scarp was measured by clinometer, and the angle proved to be quite 70 degrees. The slant was sharper than the camera makes it appear in the photograph. The only steeper gradient ascended this summer was found on the mountain soon to be described. Some mountain-fakers talk of climbing long distances at 85 degrees, but in my opinion such feats are not possible. An angle of 75 degrees may be considered the limit at which a long incline can be taken, and that will prove dangerous and strenuous enough for a hardy climber. Those who talk about long slants of 85 degrees never, I have observed, mention measuring their slopes. Soon after the great wall was ended, easier gradients brought us to the base of the mamelon west of the main peak, and here Nature gave us yet another taste of snow peculiarities in form of a 20-foot ice-wall overhung by a snow cornice fluted with massive blue icicles, below which descended the deepest of chasms. From the opening of the chasm, in all directions barring our approach, ran a series of wide most bizarre crevasses.

One porter suggested that, at last, we must give in to mountain obstacles, but Savoye laughed and shook his head. I won't bore the reader with what we did, lest he think me guilty of too many snow yarns. Suffice it to say in half an hour we stood on the snow-mamelon and saw the last thousand feet of the mountain rise up in moderate slopes above us.

This was a baffling mountain, though, even to the very top. Arriving on a ledge 20 feet from the apex, we discovered the small final cone, on the side confronting us, to be split into three giant tooth-like cornices. A short snow-slant overhanging a deep precipice separated our ledge from the cornice. Savoye, held on a good length of rope by the porters, began at once to cut his way up this. The surface was of peculiar consistency, half snow, half ice, and very hard to impress with the ice ax. After twenty minutes hacking he returned to us incased in powdery snow from head to foot. He reported that, owing to the quality of the snow, it would take nearly two hours to cut thru the cornices to the top.

In view of the advancing day and the great danger from avalanches on the descent, the question arose, Was it safe to risk it? No, we all agreed, for the mountain was virtually climbed; so, turning, we headed downward, inwardly provoked enough with the preposterous cone and its baffling trio of cornices coming just at the top, and after so many other extraordinary difficulties had been overcome. The avid explorer of new peaks, however, seldom gets all he wants, namely, perfect weather thruout an ascent and the summit, and we had reason to be well satisfied, for the weather was without a flaw, and on the last thousand feet we had secured many fine photographs, and fixed mountains on the Hispar that would aid all the further investigation of that glacier.

The last two-thirds of the descent was what might be termed a race for life in trying to reach the glacier before the usual avalanche cannonade of the afternoon began. Avalanches fell very near us at several points and we had pretty dangerous work to perform in getting thru the now-softened ice-falls, but the tents on the glacier were safely reached at 12.30, and the lower camp later on, after fifteen hours of thrilling mountain experiences. Never have I met with a peak of less than 20,000 feet so bristling with uncommon and varied snow obstacles as was this one, which was named Triple Cornice Peak.

A few years ago, from a high snow col south of the Hispar region, we saw and photographed a tall, ethereal snow-pyramid rising at a great distance above a gap in an intervening range. This we then located as being probably near the source of the Hispar Glacier, and such in reality it proved to be. At about 20 miles up the Hispar it flashed upon our view again, looming above broken snowfields north of the Hispar Pass, lifting its now more developed, more attenuated snow-spire into the blue heaven like a challenge. What a peak, and from it what a view would be obtained! Poised as it was on a huge snow-pedestal directly above the watershed of the Hispar and Biafo glaciers, its summit on a clear day would command the 75 miles of these glaciers and their surrounding mountain satellites on all sides.

During the weeks of exploring the branch glaciers, it never left my mind, and I decided, when the main work was over and a base camp at the foot of the pass established, to have my try at it.

Thus it came to pass a month later, after weeks of hard research work on the hitherto unexplored Hispar tributaries, and of existing in snow camps thru storms of fifty and sixty hours' duration, we found ourselves leaving base camp at 15,000 feet, accompanied by Savoye, the porters, headman, one servant, and fifteen coolies, carrying small tents and provisions for three days.

As with the guide and two porters I started ahead to plot out the track, I heard the coolies grumbling, and one who spoke Hindustani remarked on the "karab rasta" (bad path). If we were taking the trouble to make them a path at all on an unknown mountain they should have been satisfied, but gratitude is a non-existent word in coolie patois.

A bitter wind blew down from the Hispar Pass as we filed up to the north of it over hard, purple slopes, at that hour untouched by the sun. Two hours later, when deep in negotiation of a sérac-fall leading to a lower ridge of the mountain, the sun shining from a clear sky was so hot that fur caps and heavy coats were consigned to the depths of the rück-sacks.

Making a circuitous path around the ridge, a high snow-basin between the east and west shoulders of the peak was discovered, and this we saw was the place to camp that night, if the summit was to be gained the next day. But getting there was difficult business. An army of wicked gnomes must have been at work plowing up and making a snow hodge-podge of the lower part of this stately peak, for not ten yards of smooth surface was visible amid the maze of pinnacles, ice-fluted crevasses and torn-up slants.

We made the best way we could thru, taking care to pound our steps in the softening surface for the coolies, still a good distance in arrears. Finally a small plateau, not seen from below, was reached, and from here a very steep 800-foot snow-wall led presumably to the high basin we wished to camp in. Some one suggested lunch, it being near noon, but I replied: "Nonsense; if we stop here the coolies will refuse to go on. The wall must be taken before they arrive."

Zigzagging up in this deep, wet snow nearly to the knees was no easy work, but this task was three-quarters over when the caravan appeared on the plateau. We called down to them to hurry up, nice large steps having been made for them. Our soothing words did not, however, inspire them with confidence, and they refused to move.

At last Savoye said he would go down and help them up. This he good-naturedly did, and after parleying a time with them and the chief, as reward for his kindness, to our consternation we saw three stout Nagaris attack him with spiked sticks. But he was ready for them, and instantly, in self-defense, felled one of them to the snow with his ax. After that they subsided, and finally moved upward, the coolies who had been knocked down limping heavily behind, led by the head-man. I would add that, although the chief often beat the coolies, this was the first time a native was struck by our Europeans.

By 3.30 P.M. the tents were pitched in the eerie basin, barely safe from avalanches falling from the mountain wall between the two shoulders. These two arêtes fell straight from the pointed top of the peak in sharpest inclines over 2,000 feet. The east one was so fringed with cornices that it was absolutely unsafe, and there remained no alternative but to try the south, much steeper one, which had hitherto been deemed too hazardous.

The next morning the sky looked hazy, and we felt there would be a storm before night.

With Savoye and two porters I started out for the mountain, for, if it was climbable at all, we were likely to accomplish it before the storm

broke. Dr. Workman later left with the other porter for a lower summit
east of camp, for purposes of observation.

A few intermediate snow-fields brought us to a high wall, up the
icy surface of which steps were cut to the great shoulder that ran
apparently in sky-scraping slants clear to the top, still invisible from
where we stood. Cutting each step, we moved upward slowly, for the
arête was very narrow and ice-coated at that hour, and the precipices
on both sides were already very terrifying. After an hour's continuous
upward plodding the arête ended momentarily in a small ridge, above
which came an awkward reach of rock gendarmes.

Before attacking these we halted to breathe a bit and take in the
entrancing and widening view of glaciers and mountains. Turning my
Zeiss glass downward, my eye lit on the tents far below in the hollow.
In front of one the native was seated on the snow, enjoying the early
sunlight, wrapped in what looked suspiciously like one of our sleeping-
sacks, and composedly smoking a pipe. I handed the glass to Savoye,
who, on looking, exclaimed:

"Ah, the rascal; that's my reserve pipe and my tobacco he is smoking, for he does not own a pipe."

"And sitting in my sleep-sack doubtless," I added, turning toward
the mountain.

Who would have thought this purest of snow-pyramids was to give
us a tough stint of rock climbing? But it did, and we worked half an
hour on rock pinnacles overhanging a wild abyss, which recalled a bad
place on Zermatt's Zinal-Rothorn. As soon as these ended, a solid ice-
wall of 15 feet demanded all our skill, for only half steps could be cut,
which, when stepped upon, left most of the foot in mid air.

From this the arête led up again in increasing steepness, an endless
white line. It was here that I found the incline steeper than on the
previous ascent, reaching as near as I could make it out, about an angle
of 75 degrees. The weather was thickening in on the Hispar side, and
the sun, shining thru a haze, made the surface soft, thus adding to the
difficulty of overcoming the terrible gradient. The precipices, too, in
gruesome depths, were beyond those I recall on any mountain. One
simply had to accept the circumstance of climbing a tight rope, and
not look to right or left.

Luckily such slants lead up fast, every step being a gain in height,
and, just as all were getting quite to the end of endurance, the pitch
lessened and soon we saw the small summit rising in a sharp-corniced
cone beyond some rocks, and not ten minutes away.

We all ascended the cone, but on the very apex, which was a cornice, or snow-hood, only one at a time could stand, held on the rope by the others just below.

The view quite equaled my expectations, except that approaching bad weather marred it somewhat toward the Hispar Glacier. The whole upper Biafo, its wide source, called Snow Lake, and several great tributaries 15 miles in length, lay mapped as no map could show them, at my feet 6,000 feet below. The finest Hispar peaks and a dozen other giants of the Karakoram were visible for a few minutes, and I plainly saw that 28,000-foot colossus K2, whose sheer precipices have frowned defiance at different times on ordinary mortals, and only lately on a royal aspirant [the Duke of Abruzzi].

I saw many other sights beyond the frontier, and points that served later to make our new map superior to any existing, and then mist swept in, in rolling billows, blotting out glaciers and distant mountains, leaving us stranded on a snow-tooth, in a fluffy ocean of cloud. Before this happened, the others had seen us from the lower peak, where they stood, and Dr. Workman photographed us standing on the summit. . . .

Chilled to the bone by the swirling mist, we descended to the slight shelter of the rocks just below, where I finished my observations under cover of coats held about me by the guides, and, after a hasty meal, we left the beautiful, cloud-bound pyramid, the king of the Hispar and Biafo glaciers, that had lured me for weeks, with our hearts full of victory, for at the end of hard work we had conquered.

The descent was difficult and hazardous down the interminable arête, thru cloud and mist, but tuning all our energies to careful manipulation of every movement, we accomplished it without accident, and floundering over the final snow-fields in heavy wet snow, reached camp, where the other two greeted us with shouts of approval.

The height of this mountain, later computed, is 21,350 feet, and was named the Hispar-Biafo Watershed Peak. Altho not as high, it yielded nothing in thrilling incident and arduousness of ascent, and in magnificence of panorama, to my highest Himalayan peak of 23,300 feet.

‹Of advantage to my sex›

Annie Smith Peck
Climbs the North Peak of Huascarán, 1908

Annie Peck, an American writer and lecturer, first became fascinated with the mountains on a visit to the Alps. Seeing the Matterhorn for the first time, she felt she would never be happy until she had climbed it, but at the time she could not afford such a "great extravagance as devoting fifty dollars to a day's pleasure." Instead she contented herself with climbing less dramatic peaks, in Switzerland, Greece, and later in California, where she ascended 14,162-foot Mount Shasta, finding the exercise "delightful and invigorating." Returning to the Alps in 1895, she finally made the ascent of the Matterhorn, a well-publicized event that gained her a modicum of notoriety even though she was hardly the first woman, or even the first American woman, to make the climb. Two years later, hoping to accomplish "some deed worthy of the fame already acquired"— and having solved, at least for the time being, the chronic problem of financing her expeditions by securing the backing of the *New York World*—Peck climbed 18,885-foot Orizaba in Mexico, earning, though only for a short time, the world's altitude record for women.

Peck's next goal, as she wrote later (employing a metaphor seemingly at odds with her feminism), "was to do a little genuine exploration, to conquer a virgin peak, to attain some height where no *man* had previously stood." She would do this by climbing Bolivia's Mount Sorata, a mysterious peak rumored to be as high as twenty-five thousand feet. Her motives were complex, but prominent among them was her feminist politics:

> To establish the height of this great mountain and ascertain whether it were indeed superior to Aconcagua, generally regarded as the loftiest peak of the Western Hemisphere, to make meteorological, geological and any other observations possible in a brief visit seemed to promise a worthy contribution to science. At the same time, should the mountain rise to its greatest possibilities, to reach a higher point than any where man had previously stood seemed worthy also of a sportsman's effort; in a small way like Peary's getting a degree nearer to the North Pole. Above and beyond this, being from earliest years a firm believer in the equality of the sexes, I felt that any great achievement in any line of endeavor would be of advantage to my sex.

Peck saw climbing not only as a means of publicizing the cause of women's emancipation, but also as an activity directly beneficial to the health and well-being of the individual woman climber. She forthrightly and cogently answered the objections then being raised against mountaineering in general and women's climbing in particular, urging her sisters to ignore the contrary admonitions of men:

> Some physicians possess excess caution. One lady whose physician told her she must never walk when she could ride or stand when she could sit (he might as well have added, nor sit when she could lie down), nevertheless developed into a climber. . . . Many ladies, English, German, even French (like Mme. Caron, a typical parisienne, who would have never been suspected of such an act) climb high mountains with their husbands, and many, who have none, without.

Peck failed to climb Sorata—which in any event proved to be only slightly higher than twenty-thousand feet—but while in Peru she heard from the natives of another mountain, Huascarán, also rumored to be exceptionally high. Over the next several years she made repeated attempts on this difficult peak, finally succeeding in 1908, when, at the age of forty-eight, she attained Huascarán's 21,800-foot North Summit. The final climb taxed both Peck and her two guides to the utmost; the ensuing descent, completed in pitch darkness and high winds, was a nightmare that eventually resulted in one of the guides losing most of a hand and half of a foot to frostbite.

In the account below, excerpted from *A Search for the Apex of America*, Peck recounts that harrowing story and gives her

Annie Peck, president of the Ladies' Alpine Club, 1909. Photographer unknown. Courtesy of the Alpine Club Library.

remarks on the controversy created when Fanny Bullock Workman challenged Peck's claim to have recaptured the women's altitude record.

IN FAIRLY GOOD SEASON we encamped that night on the plain at the
top of the saddle, in two days from the snow line, a feat which I had
previously hoped with Swiss guides to be able to accomplish. The
exceptionally cold day, the coldest I had experienced in my six efforts
on this mountain, was followed by a high wind at night—an unpleasant contrast to our previous experience here, when all three nights had
been almost windless. In the early morning, I thought it wiser to
postpone our final effort till the fierce wind should abate; we should
also be in better condition following a rest from two long and hard
days' labour. Had I expected to make the attempt on this day I should
have insisted upon an earlier start. Both guides, however, though not
anxious to set out early, were in favour of going, asserting that we
might find less wind higher up, if not that we could turn back. On the
contrary, unless the wind died down altogether, it was more likely to be
worse above, and it was against my better judgment that I yielded to
their wishes.

At the late hour, for such a climb, of eight o'clock, we set forth,
myself and the two guides only, as with the two Swiss the indians [sic]
would not add to the safety of the party, probably the reverse. For the
cold ascent, I was wearing every stitch of clothing that I had brought:—
three suits of light weight woollen underwear, two pairs of tights,
canvas knickerbockers, two flannel waists, a little cardigan jacket, two
sweaters, and four pairs of woollen stockings; but as most of the
clothing was porous it was inadequate to keep out the wind, for which
I had relied upon the eskimo [sic] suit now at the bottom of a crevasse.
I had not really needed it before, nor worn it except at night. Now
when I wanted it badly, it was gone. I am often asked if my progress is
not impeded by the weight of so much clothing, to which I answer, No.
All of the articles were light, and garments which cling closely to the
body are not burdensome. I never noticed the weight at all. A skirt, on
the contrary, however short and light, anything depending from the
waist or shoulders, is some hindrance to movement and of noticeable
weight. I had not an ounce of strength to spare for superfluities, neither do I consider that an abbreviated skirt would add to the graceful-
ness of my appearance, or if it did, that this, upon the mountain, would

be of the slightest consequence: while in rock climbing the shortest skirt may be an added source of danger.

A woollen face and head mask, which I had purchased in La Paz, provided with a good nose piece as well as eye-holes, mouth-slit, and a rather superfluous painted moustache, protected my head, face, and neck from the wind. An extra one, which I had brought along, a rather better article except that it left the nose exposed, I offered to Gabriel, Rudolf having brought a hood of his own. Somewhat to my surprise, as the guides had seemed always to despise the cold and to regard my warnings as superfluous, this offer was accepted with alacrity. My hands were covered with a pair of vicuña mittens made for me in La Paz with two thicknesses of fur, one turned outside and one in. For these, until the day before, I had had no use; they now kept even my cold hands comfortable. In fact, as the sun rose higher, they became too warm and were exchanged for two pairs of wool mittens, one of which, however, did not cover the fingers. The fur mittens, being too large to go into my pocket or leather bag, were handed over to Rudolf, who was next to me, to be put into his rück-sack.

I had repeatedly warned the men of the great danger of freezing above, not so much from the actual cold as from the rarity of the air, telling them how Pelissier (one of Conway's guides), with two pairs of stockings, had had his feet frozen on Aconcagua so that they turned black, and he barely escaped losing them; how Zurbriggan, Maquignaz, and others had been frost-bitten on Aconcagua and Sorata. In spite of this, they hardly seemed to realise the necessity of so much care. They stated that their shoes would admit of but one pair of their heavy woollen stockings and seemed quite unconcerned as to the possibilities of freezing.

The men carried food and tea for luncheon (the latter I had sat up to make the night before, after the rest had gone to bed), the hypsometer to take observations, and my camera. The mercurial barometer I had left in Yungay, from misgivings that I might have to carry it if it was brought along. As there was no extra clothing of mine to transport, since I had put it all on, I ventured to ask if one of the guides could carry up the warm poncho, fearing that I might need it when we paused for luncheon or on the summit. It was rather heavy and a considerable burden at that altitude, but Gabriel said he could take it; to the fact of my extreme, apparently superfluous caution, and of Gabriel's willingness and strength, I certainly owe the possession and soundness of all my limbs, as I also owe Gabriel my life. The canteen of alcohol, which was used to light the fire of our kerosene stove, and from which also a small draught night and morning was given to the indians, was carried some distance from the tent lest the temptation to drink this in our long absence should prove too much for them. When the can was deposited in the snow, with which it was half covered to make sure that it would not blow away, I inquired, "Are you sure you can find this on our return?" Both men replied that they certainly could.

Considering the altitude our progress seemed rapid. On the slope above the camp no steps were needed, but when, after an hour or less, we turned to the left, making a long traverse among great crevasses, walls, and appalling downward slopes, it was necessary that steps should be cut all of the time. The snow was in a worse condition than before. It had been hard enough then (though softer in the middle of the day), but not so smooth. Now the severe cold had made it harder still, while the high wind had blown from the exposed slopes all of the lighter particles, leaving a surface smooth as glass, such as Gabriel said he had never seen in Switzerland except in small patches.

Coming out at length upon a ridge where we were more exposed to the wind I felt the need of my vicuña mittens which had seemed too warm below. I delayed asking for a while, hoping to come to a better standing place; but as none appeared, calling a halt I approached Rudolf, who continually held the rope for me, while Gabriel was cutting the steps, so that the delays necessary on the previous ascent were avoided. Rudolf, taking the mittens from his rück-sack with some black woven sleeves I had earlier worn on my forearms, tucked the former under one arm saying, "Which will you have first?" I had it on the end of my tongue to exclaim, "Look out you don't lose my mittens!" But like most men, the guides were rather impatient of what they considered unnecessary advice or suggestions from a woman, even an employer; so, thinking, he surely will be careful of my mittens, I refrained and said, "Give me the armlets!" A second later Rudolf cried, "I have lost one of your mittens!" I did not see it go, it slipped out at the back, but anything dropped on that smooth slope, even without the high wind, might as well have gone over a precipice.

I was angry and alarmed at his inexcusable carelessness, but it was useless to talk. I could do that after we got down, though under subsequent circumstances I never did. I hastily put my two brown woollen mittens and one red mitt on my left hand, the vicuña fur on my right which generally held the ice axe and was therefore more exposed. Onward and upward for hours we pressed, when at length we paused for luncheon being too cold and tired to eat the meat which had frozen in the rück-sack, and the almost equally hard bread; though we ate Peter's chocolate and raisins, of which we had taken an occasional nibble, each from his own pocket, all along the way. (I had found a few raisins in one of the stores and bought all they had.) The tea, too, was partially frozen in Rudolf's canteen. About two o'clock, [Rudolf] Taugwalder declared himself unable to proceed. I was for leaving him there and going on with Gabriel, but the latter urged him onward, suggesting that by leaving his rück-sack, he might be able to continue with us. This, after a short rest, he did, finding that we were going on anyway. Gabriel now carried the camera and hypsometer, in addition to the poncho, besides cutting the steps.

The latter part of the climb was especially steep. All, suffering from cold and fatigue, required frequent brief halts, though we sat down but twice on the way up and not at all at the top. At last we were approaching our goal. Rounding the apparent summit we found a broad way of the slightest grade leading gently to the northern end of the ridge, though from below, the highest point had appeared to be at the south. On the ridge, the wind was stronger than ever, and I suddenly realised that my left hand was insensible and freezing. Twitching off my mittens, I found that the hand was nearly black. Rubbing it vigorously with snow, I soon had it aching badly, which signified its restoration; but it would surely freeze again (it was now three o'clock) in the colder hours of the late afternoon and night. My over-caution in having the poncho brought up now proved my salvation. This heavy shawl or blanket, with a slit in the middle, slipped over my head, kept me fairly warm to the end, protecting my hand somewhat, as well as my whole body. At the same time, it was awkward to wear, reaching nearly to my knees, and was the cause of my slipping and almost of my death on the way down. But for the loss of my fur mitten I should not have been compelled to wear it except, as intended, on the summit.

A little farther on, Gabriel suggested our halting for the observations, as the wind might be worse at the extremity of the ridge. The slope, however, was so slight that there probably was no difference. Rudolf now untied and disappeared. I was so busy over the hypsometer that I did not notice where he went, realising only that he was not there. While, careful not to expose too much of my left hand, I shielded the hypsometer from the wind as well as I was able with the poncho, Gabriel struck match after match in vain. Once he lighted the candle, but immediately it went out. After striking twenty matches, Gabriel said, "It is useless; we must give it up." With Rudolf's assistance in holding the poncho we might have done better. But it was past three. That dread descent was before us. Sadly I packed away the instrument, believing it better to return alive, if possible, than to risk further delay. It was a great disappointment not to make the expected contribution to science; perhaps to have broken the world's record, without being able to prove it; but to return alive seemed still more desirable, even though in ignorance of the exact height to which we had attained.

Rudolf now appeared and informed me that *he* had been on to the summit, instead of remaining to assist with the hypsometer. I *was* enraged. I had told them, long before, that, as it was my expedition, I should like, as is customary, to be the first one to place my foot at the top, even though I reached it through their instrumentality. It would not lessen their honour and I was paying the bills. I had related how a few feet below the top of Mt. St. Elias, Maquignaz had stepped back and said to the Duke of the Abruzzi, "Monsieur, à vous la gloire!" And Rudolf, who with little grit had on the first attempt turned back at 16,000 feet, compelling me to make this weary climb over again, who this time had not done half so much work as Gabriel, who had wished to give up an hour below the summit, instead of remaining here with us to render assistance with the observations, had coolly walked on to the highest point! I had not *dreamed* of such an act. The disappointment may have been trivial. Of course it made no real difference to the honour to which I was entitled, but of a certain personal satisfaction, long looked forward to, I had been robbed. Once more I resolved, if ever we got down again, to give that man a piece of my mind, a large one: but after all I never did, for then he had troubles enough of his own, and words would not change the fact. Now, without a word, I went on.

Though the grade was slight, I was obliged to pause several times in the fierce wind, once leaning my head on my ice axe for a few seconds before I could continue to the goal. Gabriel stopped a short distance from the end, advising me not to go too near the edge, which I had no inclination to do, passing but a few feet beyond him. I should like to have looked down into the Llanganuco Gorge, whence I had looked up at the cliff and the thick overhanging cornice, such as impended above the east and west cliffs also. We had, therefore, kept in the centre of the broad ridge, at least 40 feet wide, it may have been more: it seemed wider than an ordinary city street. Had it been earlier

in the day, being particularly fond of precipices, and this would have
been the biggest I had ever looked down, I should have ventured near
the north edge with Gabriel holding the rope; but now I did not care
to hazard delay from the possibility of breaking through the cornice.

My first thought on reaching the goal was, "I am here at last, after
all these years; but shall we ever get down again?" I said nothing
except, "Give me the camera," and as rapidly as possible took views
towards the four quarters of the heavens, one including Gabriel. The
click of the camera did not sound just right, and fearing that I was
getting no pictures at all, I did not bother to have Gabriel try to take a
photograph of me. This I afterwards regretted, as I should like to have
preserved such a picture for my own pleasure. But in later days I was
thankful indeed that in spite of high wind and blowing snow the other
pictures did come out fairly; for it is pictures *from* the summit that tell
the tale, and not the picture of some one standing on a bit of rock or
snow which may be anywhere.

There was no pleasure here, hardly a feeling of triumph, in view of
my disappointment over the observations, and my dread of the long and
terrible descent. If ever I were safely down, there would be plenty of time
to rejoice. It was half past three, and soon would be dark. Seven hours
coming up! Would it take us as long to return? Steep rocks and icy slopes
are far more dangerous to descend, and especially perilous after dark;
with those small steps, the prospect was indeed terrifying: so without a
moment's rest we began our retreat. The summit ridge, at least a quarter
of a mile in length, was quickly traversed, at that altitude a slight change
in grade making as much difference as in bicycling.

Gabriel had led nearly all the way up, cutting most, if not all, of
the steps. Rudolf had been second, in order to hold the rope for me,
avoiding all possible delay. Going down I was roped in the middle, the
more usual position for the amateur, Rudolf at first taking the lead and
Gabriel occupying the more responsible place in the rear; for in descending, the rear is the post of honour, as that of leader in the ascent;
since the strongest of a party must be above, holding the rope in case
of a slip on the part of the amateur in front. A guide, of course, is never
expected to slip and a good one practically never does. If the rear guard
goes, as a rule all are lost.

The guides' shoes being well studded with nails they had not cared
to wear the climbing irons, to which they were unaccustomed, and
which by impeding the circulation would have made their feet colder.

My shoes were more poorly provided, as it was impossible to procure in New York such nails as are employed in the Alps. I had intended to wear the crampons which would have made them unnecessary, but on Gabriel's advice had left them below, lest my feet should be frozen, as the one previously touched by the frost would have greater liability.

At the end of the ridge difficulties began. A smooth slope of 60 degrees is never pleasant. From the beginning of the descent I greatly feared the outcome, but we had to go down and the faster we could go, yet carefully, the better. Presently I saw something black fly away: one of Rudolf's mittens. One might suppose that after losing mine he would have been the more careful of his own. When I inquired afterwards how he came to lose it, he said he laid it down on that icy slope to fasten his shoe. Of course the wind blew it away. Later I learned that after dark he lost the second mitten. This he said was in trying to change from one hand to the other. He thought he had hold of it, but his hand being numb, he could not feel it, and this went also. If he had spoken we should have halted, so that he could make sure. His carelessness seems incredible and inexcusable, and brought disastrous consequences to himself and nearly to us all, almost costing our lives. Probably I should not have slipped, had I not been obliged on account of the loss of my fur mittens to wear the poncho which occasionally prevented my seeing the steps. Certainly Rudolf himself would not have slipped any more than Gabriel, if his hands had not been frozen and himself chilled through, so that one foot froze also; thus his footing was insecure and his grip on his ice axe less firm. It seems almost a miracle that he slipped only once and that we at last got down alive. His carelessness may perhaps be explained by the fact of his being so much affected by the altitude that it rendered him stupid, as below he had seemed as thoughtful and as careful as Gabriel. The latter, however, I had regarded as a trifle the more intelligent, as he was evidently the stronger.

On this steep slope, I deeply regretted the absence of my climbing irons, for the steps were small indeed. On the Jungfrau those made by my guide Baumann were very large, requiring from ten to twenty blows; but this would never do on the much longer slope of Huascarán. Two or three hacks for each were all that Gabriel could give, so they were not half as large as his shoes, little more than toe-holes. They did well enough going up but not on the way down. While zigzagging I missed a step, sat down and slid a few feet, but Gabriel above was holding the rope tight and I easily regained my footing.

Some time after dark it seemed advisable for Gabriel to take the lead (such matters of course I left to them), perhaps because he was more familiar with the way or could see better on the long sloping traverse across the wide face of the mountain in the midst of caverns, crevasses, and those dreadful slopes and precipices; yet as a slide any-where would have been fatal, one place was just as bad as another, except as some parts were steeper. Gabriel estimated the incline as from 40 degrees to 60 degrees through the greater part of the distance. I had brought with me a clinometer, but never had time and strength to use it. I had been on measured slopes of 42 degrees and 53 degrees on my first mountain, and judging from these, had never afterwards over-estimated any that had been capable of verification. My opinion here coincides with Gabriel's. If anyone should not accept it, the matter is of little consequence as compared with the altitude, which unfortunately I had been obliged to leave unmeasured. But that could be determined at a later date. Whatever it might be, the *fact* of my ascent would stand.

My recollection of the descent is as of a horrible nightmare, though such I never experienced. The little moon seemed always at my back, casting a shadow over the place where I must step. The poncho would sway in the wind, and, with my motion as I was in the act of stepping, would sometimes conceal the spot where my foot should be placed. Although my eye for distance is good, my foot once missed the step, slipping then on the smooth slope so that I fell, as usual in a sitting posture, crying out at the same time to warn the guides. I expected nothing serious, but to my horror, I did not remain where I was. Still sitting I began to slide down that glassy, ghastly incline. As we were all nearly in the same line, I slid at least fifteen feet before coming to a halt, when checked by the rope. Now to get back! The guides called to me to get up, but being all in a heap, with the rope tight around my waist, I was unable to move. The guides therefore came together just above and hauled me up the slope. Thankful again to be in the line of the steps, though now more alarmed than ever, I went onward, resolved to be more careful. But again I slipped, and again slid far below. While from the beginning of the descent, I had greatly feared the outcome, after these slips my terror increased. Sev-eral times I declared that we should never get down alive. I begged Gabriel to stop for the night and make a cave in the snow, but, saying this was impossible, he continued without a pause. The snow indeed was too hard, yet in some cavern or crevasse I thought we could find shelter from the wind. Gabriel afterwards asserted that if we had stopped we should all have frozen to death.

Again and again I slipped, five or six times altogether, but always Gabriel held his ground firmly. Always, too, I clung to my ice axe; so to his shout, "Have you your axe?" I could respond in the affirmative, and sometimes with it could help myself back again. Once when I had slipped, I was astonished to see Rudolf dart by me, wondering how he could help me by running far below. Afterwards I learned, that with my pull he, too, had slipped and Gabriel's strong arm alone saved us all from destruction. Had he given way, after sliding some distance we should all have dropped off thousands of feet below. When he saw Rudolf go, Gabriel thought for a moment that we were all lost; but his axe was well placed with the rope around it, and although two fingers were caught between the rope and the ice axe, knowing it was life or death he stood firm until Rudolf recovered himself. Otherwise, Gabriel said afterwards, he never despaired but thought only of going on. Rudolf, however, to my great astonishment, for I had supposed I was the only one who was frightened, confessed later that he never expected to get down alive.

The cold and fatigue, the darkness and shadow, the poncho blowing before me, the absence of climbing irons, the small steps, the steep glassy slopes, presented an extraordinary combination of difficulties. It seemed that the way would never end. I tried to comfort myself with the reflection that accidents do not run in our family, that nothing serious, more than broken ribs or knee-pan—these not in climbing—ever *had* happened to me; but also I was aware that people do not generally die but once. I said to myself, for the first time in my life, I *must* keep cool and do my best, and so I did; but after several of those horrible slides—Well, there was nothing to do but to plod along.

At last, at last—! Before I was aware that we had emerged from among those terrible abysses to the slope above the tent, Gabriel said "Now we are safe; and if you like you can slide." What a tremendous relief! I sat down happily, Gabriel walking ahead and guiding me with the rope. At first it was fun, then I went too fast, bobbing here and there, bumping, floundering, finally turning around, sliding on my back, and giving my head a hard whack before I came to a halt. However, we were nearly down and walked on to the tent where we arrived at half past ten, thankful for rest and shelter. There was nothing to drink, we were too tired to eat or sleep, but glad indeed to sit down in safety, too fatigued at first even to lie down. Poor Rudolf! His hands were badly frozen, his fingers black, the left hand worse than the right. He was rubbing them weakly with snow, first one, then the other. I told him he should rub them harder to get up circulation; I felt I ought to it myself, but somehow sat there and did not. . . .

I was greatly grieved to learn afterwards in Lima that it was finally necessary to amputate most of [Rudolf] Taugwalder's left hand, a finger of his right, and half of one foot. He was unable to travel until December, when the men rode down to Samanco and sailed to Callao, where they took the steamer for Panama and New York, returning in January to their homes in Zermatt. The well-known surgeon, Dr. William Tod Helmuth, kindly examined Rudolf in New York City, and I was glad to hear him say that undoubtedly he had received suitable attention and that the operations, especially the very difficult one on his foot, had been excellently performed.

Concerning the altitude of Mt. Huascarán, in regard to which there has been a rather one-sided controversy, a few words must be said. That I ever asserted the height of the mountain to be 24,000 feet is a deliberate misstatement, to which my articles published in *Harper's Magazine* for January, 1909, and in the *Bulletin* of the American Geographical Society for June of the same year bear witness. . . .

Solely in the interest of science, it is said, an expedition of three French engineers was sent from Paris to Peru to secure the altitude of this one mountain. Apparently the work was done with an extreme care which presupposes accurate measurement; yet $13,000 seems a large sum to spend for the triangulation of a single mountain which it cost but $3,000 to climb. With $1,000 more for my expedition, I should have been able with an assistant to triangulate the peak myself. With $12,000 additional I could have triangulated and climbed many mountains and accomplished other valuable exploration. The figures given as the result of this triangulation are 21,812 feet for the north peak and 22,187 for the south. Though it would thus appear that Huascarán is not so lofty as I had hoped, my ten long years of effort had culminated in the conquest of a mountain at least 1,500 feet higher than Mt. McKinley, and 2,500 feet higher than any man residing in the United States had climbed. With this I must be content until opportunity is offered to investigate some other possibilities in regard to the Apex of America.

«I would lose my reputation»

Freda du Faur and the New Zealand Alps, 1909

Freda du Faur grew up in the Australian bush, "miles from any-where," as she puts it in the excerpt below, and "happily igno-rant of both mountains and mountaineering." In 1906, she made her first visit to New Zealand's Southern Alps, where a mountaineering center had recently been established and where she met the renowned guide Peter Graham. She did not do any serious climbing on this first visit, but she was determined to re-turn to give the sport a try. When she did so, in 1908, she dis-covered she had a remarkable aptitude and quickly developed into a competent alpinist. In 1910, in just her third real season as a climber, she ascended the highest peak in the range, 12,800-foot Mount Cook, becoming the first woman to do so. Three years later she returned and, with Peter Graham and Dave Thomas, made the first successful crossing of Mount Cook's three distinct summits, the "Grand Traverse" that is still considered one of the most impressive accomplishments in New Zealand climbing.

In the account below, excerpted from *The Conquest of Mount Cook*, Du Faur recounts how she first fell in love with the Southern Alps—and how she overcame the disapprobation of her peers.

I HAVE BEEN ASKED so often "What made you take up mountaineer-ing?" that perhaps it will be wise to devote the first few pages of this book to answering the oft-repeated question, and endeavouring to explain the fascination the mountains exercise over me.

To begin with, I sincerely believe that the true mountaineer, like the poet, is born, not made. The details of their craft both of course must learn, but the overmastering love of the mountains is something which wells up from within and will not be denied. An unsympathetic environment and want of opportunity may keep this love hidden from even its possessor; but alter the environment and give the opportunity and the climber will climb as naturally as the sparks fly upward.

The majority of my readers will know that Australia possesses no permanently snow-clad mountains; so the average Australian may perhaps never see snow and ice, and has nothing in his environment to encourage a love of mountaineering. My own life was no exception to this rule. I lived in the bush happily ignorant of both mountains and mountaineering. My home from the age of seventeen was situated four miles from anywhere, on the edge of a twenty-five miles Government reserve. This reserve, left absolutely in a state of nature, is a series of ridges with valleys of from 300 to 400 feet in depth on either side. These ridges and valleys are for the most part unexplored. They are of sandstone formation, and are a regular paradise for wild flowers. Lured by the flowers, I explored ridge and valley for miles, usually with no other companion than a hound, who deserted me whenever so inclined, to chase iguanas, 'possums, and native bears. During five years of scrambling I gained a very considerable knowledge of rock-climbing.

Indeed, I faced some very pretty problems without either the moral or material support of a rope or a companion. The support was all given to my dog, who would frequently sit and howl dismally on the top of a cliff that I had just succeeded in scrambling down, until I returned and found an easier road for him or deserted him until he found a way for himself. Besides rock-craft I developed a love of exploring and adventure, and a self-reliance which caused my parents some alarm. However, the expected never happened: I neither broke my neck, sprained my ankle, nor was bitten by a snake, but always returned home intact; so they ceased to worry, and left me to my own devices, which all unconsciously laid the foundation of my mountaineering career.

For some years I spent my summers in the North Island of New Zealand, but I don't remember ever hearing of the Southern Alps. I used to strain my eyes to see Mount Egmont, and on a clear morning was sometimes rewarded by the glimpse of a white pyramid across the sea: but it was too ethereal and far away to wake any mountaineering ambitions.

In 1906 I went south for the first time, to see the Christchurch Exhibition. There I saw my first picture of Mount Cook, and met people who had visited the Southern Alps. As my interest in the mountains increased, the charms of the exhibition waned, and I decided to go to the mountains. I had no thought of climbing, I was merely filled with curiosity to see something that was quite outside my experience, so at the end of December I set out.

People who live amongst the mountains all their lives, who have watched them at sunrise and sunset, in midday heat or moonlight glow, love them, I believe, as they love the sun and flowers, and take them as much for granted. They have no conception how the first sight of them strikes to the very heart-strings of that less fortunate individual, the hill-lover who lives in a mountainless country. From the moment my eyes rested on the snow-clad alps I worshipped their beauty and was filled with a passionate longing to touch those shining snows, to climb to their heights of silence and solitude, and feel myself one with the mighty forces around me. The great peaks towering into the sky before me touched a chord that all the wonders of my own land had never set vibrating, and filled a blank of whose very existence I had been unconscious. Many people realize the grandeur and beauty of the mountains, who are quite content to admire them from a distance, if strenuous physical exertion is the price they must pay for a nearer acquaintance. My chief desire as I gazed at them was to reach the snow and bury my hands in its wonderful whiteness, and dig and dig till my snow-starved Australian soul was satisfied that all this wonder of white was real and would not vanish at the touch.

To a restless, imaginative nature the fascination of the unknown is very great; from my childhood I never saw a distant range without longing to know what lay on the other side. So in the mountains the mere fact of a few thousand feet of rock and snow impeding my view was a direct challenge to climb and see what lay behind it. It is as natural to me to wish to climb as it is for the average New Zealander to be satisfied with peaceful contemplation from a distance.

The night of my arrival at the Hermitage the chief guide, Peter Graham, was introduced to me. Knowing his reputation as a fine and enthusiastic mountaineer, I felt sure that he, at least, would understand my craving for a nearer acquaintance with the mountains. I asked him what it was possible for a novice to attempt. After a few questions as to my walking capabilities, he suggested that I should accompany a party he was taking up the Sealy Range. Only an inci-

dent here and there remains of that climb. Firstly, I remember fulfilling
my desire to dig in the snow (at the expense of a pair of very sunburnt
hands) and joyously playing with it while the wiser members of the
party looked on. Likewise I remember a long, long snow slope, up
which we toiled in a burning sun, never seeming to get any nearer to
the top. At length, when the summit came in sight, the others were so
slow I could not contain my curiosity; so I struck out for myself instead
of following in Graham's footsteps. Soon I stood alone on the crest of
the range, and felt for the first time that wonderful thrill of happiness
and triumph which repays the mountaineer in one moment for hours
of toil and hardship. On the descent I experienced my first glissade; it
was rather a steep slope, and I arrived at the bottom wrong side up, and
inconveniently filled with snow. These facts, however, did not deter me
from tramping back to the top just for the pleasure of doing the same
thing all over again. At the end of the day I returned to the hotel fully
convinced that earth held no greater joy than to be a mountaineer.

My day in the snows had taught me several things, but chief of
them was the knowledge that I could never be content to worship the
mountains from a distance. This raised the question: Had I, besides the
inborn love of climbing, the other requirements of a mountaineer?
Had I the physical strength, courage, endurance, and perseverance
without which nothing worth doing could be accomplished? My time
was so limited that it was useless to expect to find the answers to these
questions. So I decided to return and test my capabilities at a later
date.

Fate, in the shape of an urgent cablegram, made it necessary for
me to leave even sooner than I had expected, and I returned home
almost at once.

It was two years before I was able to take a holiday again. When
the chance came I set out for the Southern Alps with my enthusiasm
by no means impaired. From various causes my holiday was limited to a
fortnight, but short though it was it was long enough to settle the
question of my capabilities. I was fortunate in always going out with
parties that were under the charge of the chief guide, and which
usually included no other woman. Very soon Graham realized that I
was always the most enthusiastic, and often the fittest of the party at
the end of the day, so he began to watch me carefully. One day three of
us climbed with him to a pass immediately beneath the third summit
of Mount Cook; it was the highest point to which I had ascended. As I
stood on the summit I felt that my question was answered. I could do

what I would. Silently I gazed at the thin, jagged ridge in front of me leading up to Mount Cook. Then and there I decided I would be a real mountaineer, and some day be the first woman to climb Mount Cook. When I had made this decision I was half afraid of it. I knew the history of every expedition hitherto undertaken; I knew how trained men and guides had been beaten back time and again, and how fierce was the struggle of those few who had succeeded. Thinking of these things I wondered at my own presumption, and wisely decided to say nothing of my ambitions. On our return I interviewed Graham, and said I would like to come back the following year and do some high climbing if he considered I was fit for it, and would undertake to train me in snow and ice work, of which I knew nothing. He willingly agreed to do so, saying he saw no reason why I should not make a mountaineer. Mount Cook was never mentioned by either of us, and the next day I left for Sidney.

In the spring of 1909 I had word from Graham that if I still wished to keep to our arrangement of the previous year I could not do better than come over early in the season before the Christmas rush of tourists made serious demands upon his time.

Nothing loath, I made my arrangements, and on December 6th left for Lyttelton by the s.s. *Marama*. I am ever unhappy at sea, so the less said of the five days' voyage the better. The fact that I willingly undergo such days of misery every year may give some idea of how deep is my devotion to New Zealand.

Once on land again I ceased to feel so wilted, and by the time the south-bound train moved slowly out of Christchurch life was worth living once more, and the rattle of the wheels resolved itself into a joyous refrain, "Mountain bound, mountain bound!" The houses were soon left behind, and the wide, barless windows framed picture after picture. First, a field of growing grain, swaying before the soft spring breeze; bounded by hedges of golden gorse and protected by break-winds of slender poplars standing like sentinels against the sky-line. Then a wide, grey river-bed, with silvery streams, curling and twisting through its great expanse; here and there shone patches of vivid gold, where broom and gorse turned the grey wilderness to a patch of burning colour. The miles flew past, and through the window was wafted the unmistakable salt savour of the sea; marshes stretched on either hand leading to the curved grey beach and vivid emerald waters of the little seaport of Timaru, where a long, straight breakwater stretches out into the ocean, affording sole protection to all the vessels rocking so peacefully at the wharves. After half an hour's wait at Timaru we were transferred into the little train that conveyed us to the end of the railway at Fairlie. A peaceful, placid little train this, which pursued its way with many pauses through fertile hills and valleys—hills so steep that one wondered how the ploughman guided his team and prepared the land for the wheat, oats, and clover that waved on either hand.

The Hermitage is beautifully situated at an altitude of 2,510 feet near the terminal face of the Muller Glacier, which winds in a northerly direction under Mount Sefton and the other peaks of the dividing range. The front of the hotel affords a beautiful view of Mount Sefton, and a few minutes' walk from the back brings one to a fine viewpoint for Mount Cook. We arrived about 5.30 P.M., and I spent the hours till dinner-time in wandering about renewing my acquaintance with the mountains.

I found that Graham was away in charge of a party up the Tasman Glacier and would not be back until the following evening, and until his return I could make no plans as to the course of my future training. The following day was wet, so I had an enforced rest, which no doubt did me good after my week's traveling. Graham came back in the evening and suggested a couple of minor excursions to put me in touch with the mountains again. The first of these took the form of a traverse of Mount Kinsey and Mount Wakefield. We had a glorious day, and returned home after ten hours' scramble sunburned, hungry, and happy. This climb had the effect of convincing Graham that I was in excellent condition and fit to tackle bigger things without more preliminaries.

We decided therefore to climb Mount Sealy on the first fine day, the weather having turned bad after our day on Mount Kinsey. Mount Sealy requires a bivouac, as it is some distance from the Hermitage, and there are no huts in that direction. This fact did not trouble me, but I soon learnt to my sorrow that I had to reckon with the other people in the house. As I was a girl, travelling alone, the women in the house apparently considered themselves more or less responsible for my actions. On Mount Kinsey I had been accompanied by a tourist who wished to join our party. As soon as I cheerfully announced, when asked, that I was going to climb Mount Sealy alone with a guide, I found myself up against all the cherished conventions of the middle-aged. In vain I argued and pointed out that I had come to the mountains to climb, not to sit on the veranda and admire the view. If I were to limit my climbs to occasions on which I could induce another woman or man to accompany me, I might as well take the next boat home. At the moment there was no one in the hotel who could or would climb Mount Sealy; there was not the ghost of a climber on the premises, only women who found a two-mile walk quite sufficient for their powers. This they could not deny, but they assured me in all seriousness that if I went out alone with a guide I would lose my reputation.

The fact that the guide in question was Peter Graham, whose reputation as a man was one at which the most rigid moralist could not cavil, made no difference. They acknowledged it was true, but seemed absolutely incapable of applying it to the facts of the case. One old lady implored me with tears in her eyes not to "spoil my life for so small a thing as climbing a mountain." I declined gently but firmly to believe that it would be spoilt, and added, with some heat I am afraid, that if my reputation was so fragile a thing that it would not bear such a test, then I would be very well rid of a useless article. Though not convincing me that I was doing anything wrong, they had succeeded in worrying me considerably. I turned over plans in my mind, seeking a way out of the difficulty; for about ten minutes I almost succeeded in wishing that I possessed that useful appendage to a woman climber, a husband. However, I concluded sadly that even if I possessed him he would probably consider climbing unfeminine, and so my last state might be worse than my first, and the "possible he" was dismissed as unhelpful at this crisis of my affairs. Instead I sought out Graham and told him that the female population was holding up hands of horror, and asked what we were going to do about it. He suggested a compromise in the shape of taking a porter with us. I agreed to this, but felt vindictive when I thought of the extra expense entailed, and threatened to send the bill into my tormentors. Graham agreed that advice was cheap and that they might feel rather different if they were asked £1 a day for it. However, it seemed like the thin edge of the wedge, and later I would probably be beyond their advice. I sighed, not for the first time in my existence, over the limits imposed upon me by the mere fact that I was unfortunate enough to be born a woman. I would like to see a man asked to pay for something he neither needed nor wanted, when he had been hoarding up every penny so that he need not be cramped for want of funds. I don't wish to pose as a martyr, but merely to point out the disadvantages of being a woman pioneer even in the colonies, where we are supposed to be so much less conventional than elsewhere. I was the first unmarried woman who had wanted to climb in New Zealand, and in consequence I received all the hard knocks until one day when I awoke more or less famous in the mountaineering world, after which I could and did do exactly as seemed to me best.

Fortunately in this world, the wonder of one day is taken as a matter of course the next; so now, five years after my first fight for individual freedom, the girl climber at the Hermitage need expect nothing worse than raised eyebrows when she starts out unchaperoned and clad in climbing costume. It is some consolation to have achieved as much as this, and to have blazed one more little path through ignorance and convention, and added one tiny spark to the ever-growing beacon lighted by the women of this generation to help their fellow-travellers climb out of the dark woods and valleys of conventional tradition and gain the fresh, invigorating air and wider viewpoint of the mountain-tops.

«A secret, cherished history»

Dorothy Pilley on Her Discovery of Climbing, 1910–20

A founding member of the Pinnacle Club and "probably the outstanding woman climber of the early 1920s," Dorothy Pilley was initiated into climbing on her native British crags. She was part of a generation that increasingly saw rock climbing not only as training for the snowpeaks of the Alps and other ranges but also as an intriguing and demanding sport in itself. When she did begin to visit the Alps, she was already so skilled that she succeeded on the notorious Grépon that first season. During her second season, in 1921, with her friends Annie Wells and Lilian Bray but no men on the rope, she climbed the 10,328-foot Mittaghorn—not a particularly difficult climb, but a fore-shadowing of Miriam O'Brien's spectacular *cordée féminine* ascents of the later 1920s.

Pilley's best season—the one she referred to as the "Great Year"—came in 1928. She had recently married the literary critic I. A. Richards, whom she first met in 1921 in the Alps and who was himself an accomplished climber. For their honeymoon, the couple succeeded in climbing one of the great "unsolved problems" of the Alps, the North Ridge of the Dent Blanche. Pilley wrote later that at one particularly steep passage, where she and her new husband were crowded together onto a tiny stance on the otherwise vertical cliff, clinging to a single handhold scarcely sufficient for one, their guide looked them over and deadpanned, "Ah, *les amoureaux!*"

A respected journalist and writer, Pilley traveled widely in China and became an authority on Chinese art and religion. She had a varied circle of friends that at times included T. S.

Dorothy E. Pilley. Date and photographer unknown. Courtesy of the
Alpine Club Library.

Eliot and Adrienne Rich. Her autobiography, *Climbing Days,*
first published in 1935, is an acknowledged classic of the mountaineering canon. Gracefully written, by turns sensitive and entertaining, it brilliantly evokes the subtle beauty of the sport
and the intense power it can exercise over its practitioners. At
the end of one of her early seasons, for example, she wrote poi-
gnantly of the sense of division and loss she felt upon returning
to her more conventional life in the city:

> How the contrast shook one! To go back to gloves and high-heeled
> shoes, pavements and taxicabs. Walking with an umbrella in Pica-
> dilly one felt as though with a little more strain one could become a
> case of divided personality. This time yesterday! One lay munching
> a dry sandwich on a rocky ledge, plucking at a patch of lichen and
> listening to the distant roar of the white Ogwen Falls. It wavered,
> faded, and grew again louder as the breeze caught it. What had such
> moments to do with to-day, and what reckoning could compare the
> personality now moving through the noisy street on her way to
> meet people who knew her in one guise only, with that other
> personality that came to life only among such a different order of
> existence and was known only to such other minds and assessed by
> them for such other qualities. The strangeness of the dual life made,
> in those days, a cleft, a division in my mind that I struggled in vain
> to build some bridge across. Kind, firm friends would say, "All good
> things come to an end," or, "You can't expect all life to be a holi-
> day." But to me, and to climbers before and after me, this was no
> question of holidays. It went down into the very form and fabric of
> myself.

Pilley continued climbing until 1958, when an accident
caused by a drunken driver left her with a broken hip. "Afterwards," she wrote, "well, the scale of the Alps, and of much
else, is strangely changed." She died in 1986. In the excerpt below, reprinted from the chapter she titled "Initiation" in *Climbing Days,* Pilley recalls her earliest climbs.

LONG AGO a young soldier gave a school-girl a novel with a vivid
description of the Brenva Route of Mont Blanc—modelled on Moore's
account in his Diary. The knife-edge ice ridge, the desperate night on
the slope, the earlier pictures from *Running Water* of the Pavillon de
Lognan and the Aiguille d'Argentière mingled in her mind with fairy-
tale Glass Mountains, Mountains of the Moon, K'un Lun Western
Paradises—abodes of ice-princesses from which ordinary mortals are
dragged back by the hair. A strange, now unrecapturable farrago of

fantasies, remaining perhaps a vague haunting background to all my mountain experiences.

The first entry of these dreams into actuality came with a visit to Beddgelert. In place of the pleasant family holidays by the sea—the esplanades, the sands, the young "nuts" with their ties and canes, the warblings of the fair young tenor at the Pierrots, in his beautifully creased white flannels and 'Varsity blazer—came the grey village street, the tawny blotches of the bracken, the reeds swaying in the breeze round the shores of Llyn Dinas, the smell of the moss and the peat. What did it matter that we went up Craig-y-Llan in long skirts and in what the boot-sellers regard as feminine walking boots? We found our way down by the mine-shafts in the dark. It was like waking up from a half sleep with the senses cleared, the self released. It was as if I had never seen anything before to strike me as beautiful. The Aberglaslyn Pass seemed the limiting possibility of awful grandeur. Sheer rock walls were edged with sentinel trees in dark silhouette against the sky. Wordsworth does not exaggerate at all; the hills, the cliffs, the cataracts haunt the mind that first gives itself to them "like a passion". I was distraught by the feelings that arose. They came with a shock of utter newness upon me, and a mossy rock would stare at me like a stranger until nothing in the world seemed to matter except my desperate attempts to discover what its significance could be. Hours passed trying to describe, in a note-book, the flowing water, clear, softly lipping over stones with a chase of fleecy foam-mice running out from under them over amber and cat's-eye depths. They were both a joy and a pain, an endless excitement and an endless disappointment. I was helpless before these feelings and knew my helplessness.

The visit culminated in a stupendous ascent of Snowdon. It was all due to a grandfatherly schoolmaster, bearded and Ruskinesque, with a flock of thirty little boys. To us all, the ascent of the highest mountain in England and Wales was a terrifying feat. Our bearded senior fortunately had Alpine experience to comfort us, but when, on reaching the narrow saddle just below the Llechog ridge (as Baedeker might say "fit only for adepts with strong heads"), he developed vertigo and could go no further, our sense of adventure was redoubled. Breathlessly we scampered up to the summit. Idle to pretend I remember the view. All that comes to the mind is a memory of effort and achievement, intoxicating ginger-beer at fourpence a bottle, a picture of our old friend sitting on the slope by the saddle, and the exact forms of the grey spiky rocks about him with the moss between them.

Next year in the spring the mountains had their chance to lay hold of me for good. Work with the Soldiers' and Sailors' Families Association and an attempt to become an Egyptologist led to a two-months rest. Hieroglyphics had been too much for the eyes. With a small cottage in Beddgelert as our base, my school friend, Winifred Ellerman, a tireless and imaginative walker, and I ranged the surrounding mountains. On Moel Hebog, when we reached the last shale slope, we halted—not knowing whether it was not the safest plan to crawl over the slippery surface on all fours. It seemed to us we should slide down with the whole mountain. What moments of terror we enjoyed! After trying it gingerly we walked up boldly, to be welcomed as courageous mountaineers by hotel acquaintances on the summit. A fateful meeting, for we were invited to make with them the circuit of the Moel Wynns over to Festiniog and back—which we counted thirty miles. After this we were singled out as "indefatigables". Herbert Carr, then beginning his very active and enterprising climbing career, asked us to come with him up a *real* climb—the Y Gully and Notch Arête of Tryfan. Tryfan, the grim guardian of the upper Nant Ffrancon, the rockiest peak south of the Tweed and the only Welsh mountain that cannot be climbed without using the hands; what a chance! I knew then that I should be for ever grateful to him. Never shall I forget my breathless anticipations. All night I lay sleepless with excitement.

As we rounded the bend of the road above Capel Curig and first caught sight of it, I remember trembling with delight and fear. The two summit rocks (ten feet high) were to me, as to so many others before and after me, two humans spell-bound in eternal conversation. I was told that they were called Adam and Eve and that a climber's duty was to spring lightly from one to the other. I asked naïvely (I have since blushed to recall) why one should not be content with ascending the mountain by the easiest route. The question to the non-climber or "mere walker" seems natural and proper enough; but I was soon to learn the climber's answer. In fact, from that day on, "climbing" was to become a word with a specialized meaning not to be used just for walking up steep slopes. The climber speaks generally of "going up Snowdon" when he follows the zigzags of the path and "climbs" only when he uses his hands as well as his feet.

When I got out of the car by the tenth milestone from Bangor on the Ogwen lakeside—for the first of how many times?—the mountain seemed to hang over our heads. We wound up the boulder-strewn slope to the foot of the climb and then I made my first acquaintance with scree. Harmless substance enough but singularly terrifying to the un-initiated. The mountaineer knows that if he jumps on to that rock scrap-heap it will slide with him about a foot and then settle down till he jumps again. But the beginner feels sure that he will start sliding and never stop till he lies a mangled body at the bottom. So the heroes of Crockett or Rider Haggard novels have their most ghastly escapes on scree-slopes. And years later I recall that an American friend, after coming gallantly and recklessly up an east-face climb on Tryfan, halted at this very scree funnel, to declare that it "sure was a mighty mean slope to fall down".

This danger past, the climb that followed showed no terrors. It was a journey full of discoveries as to how well the body fits the rocks, how perfectly hand- and foot-hold are apportioned to the climber's needs. I was later to find out that this was a peculiarity of Tryfan rather than of climbing as practised by modern experts. In the exhilaration of these discoveries the climb seemed over before it had properly started. I felt like a child when the curtain goes down at the pantomime. Why hadn't I enjoyed it ten times more while it was on? Every moment was glorious and as quickly gone. The cold wind was whistling round Adam and Eve by the time we reached the summit. It persuaded half the party to walk down to the car. Herbert Carr and I descended the South Gully and, undamped, rushed off in the dusk to scramble up the windswept Bristly Ridge, that comes down Glyder Fach to Bwlch Try-fan, and make our way over to Pen-y-Gwryd. If we had conquered the hardest climb in the district we could not have rejoiced more. "Moun-tain madness" had me now for ever in its grasp.

Followed four days of ecstatic climbing in perfect weather. Blue-bells were in the woods and ranunculus in the swamps as we passed on our way up to the cliffs. They were lovely beyond belief; but my thoughts were mainly on *footholds* and *handholds*. Each *pitch* or passage of the climb seemed as important as the Battle of Waterloo. The Horseshoe of Snowdon for the first time, the Parson's Nose, the Crazy Pinnacle Gully on Crib Goch, and a day on the Nantle Y Garn, were each, as a member of the party was fond of repeating, "a day which will live". Y Garn gave a lesson which was to prove useful. It is a mountain with a bad reputation for large, loose, treacherous blocks. In 1910 Anton Stoop, the brilliant young Swiss climber, was killed there. He was lowering himself over a huge block that two heavier men had first descended without its showing signs of danger. It heeled out with him and carried him down helpless. Knowing this story, we treated everything with our utmost care. Nevertheless, just as the party left a terrace of poised blocks, one of them, like a slice out of a cheese, slid away without warning. The crash and the sulphurous smell shook us violently and reaffirmed the need for caution.

After this I was alone in the hills for some weeks. It was now impossible for me to keep away from the high ridges. I wandered round the Horseshoe of Snowdon alone and with any party that would follow me. Greatly venturing, I went up "Lockwood's Chimney", a dark chasm under Pen-y-Gwryd, alone. With what wild glory in my heart did I wriggle out of the hole and find myself in the sunlight on the giddy upper wall. I induced a large, not too willing party of novices to come up the Great Gully of Clogwyn-y-Garnedd after me. By this time I had become the proud possessor of an Alpine rope (from Beale's, with a red strand through it!). How I had studied all the particulars about its strength in George Abraham's *The Complete Mountaineer*. How ashamed I was of its brilliant newness; it had to be muddied at all costs. A first pair of climbing boots shine like twin stars in memory, too. They were large, much too heavy and too high in the leg, but the whole village used to come to see them. I still did not dare to go about Beddgelert without a skirt, and was rather balloony in a thick, full pair of tweed knickerbockers under a billowy tweed skirt which I put in the sack at the foot of the climb. I was particularly careful never to hide it under a rock, having read of Mrs. Aubrey Le Blond's adventure on the Rothorn. How I admired that great woman climber's exploit. To traverse the Rothorn from Zermatt nearly down to Zinal and then— discovering that her skirt had been left on the summit—to go all the way back again and down to Zermatt to round the day off! What an exemplar to contemplate when the ridge of Crib-y-Ddysgl seemed long and narrow in the windy morning.

June came and a week's leave for Herbert Carr. We were both more full of enthusiasm and energy than ever. Our joint ambition, we hardly dared to whisper it, was the conquest of Lliwedd. It is impossible, now that Lliwedd climbs have become such well-known ground, to recapture all the awe and fascination which hung about them then. Though from the shores by Llydaw on any cloudy day the gloom of those black precipices can still daunt the heart. The water laps against the boulders in an inhuman, endless song. The wind streaks the surface with thin lines of foam. Across Llydaw, a loose strip of rusty corrugated-iron roof bangs drearily in the gusts and a sheep baas as though in anguish. There in the hollow of the Cwm the dark smooth walls of Lliwedd tower up. The men who made those steeps their playground seemed to me a race of giants—mysterious beings hardly of this world, undaunt-able, diamond-nerved and steel-sinewed. Many a time I had peered down from the sharp crest, to shudder at the curve of its terrific slabs. To the lay eye there seems no room for a human foot upon it. That men could have worked their way up by scores of routes was incredible. Most of all when clouds swept down from Y Wyddfa and the gulf under the crags seemed bottomless. The precipice of Lliwedd then might be ten instead of merely one thousand feet high.

But there were no clouds about when we set out. It was hot walking in my thick tweeds across the green slopes above the lake. The long swamp grass rustled dry underfoot; the sunlight cut out the ribs of the cliff above the Horned Crag, showing the Terminal Arête in sharp definition against the blackness of the shadowed gullies. We came into the shade on the litter of scree at the foot as though into a cave of secluded mysteries. Lliwedd from here heels over—like a *Titanic* just about to take its plunge. The immense parallel sweeping lines of its buttresses, echoed by every one of their scores of minor ridges, tilt over together. This heel does not disguise the steepness of the cliff, it gives it indeed an extra touch of loftiness (as of a ship's spars) from the scree and is one of the secrets of the mountain's hold on the imagination. Climbing on it you can never for a moment forget where you are. We put on the rope and set to work somewhere on the West Peak. I doubt if I could find the exact point to-day.

It was the first time we had been on ground which felt really *steep*. Or rather, it altered our conception of steepness for us. On Tryfan you halt on ample ledges—places where you can walk about and sit down with a choice of comfortable positions. On Lliwedd, for long stretches at a time, when you halt you have to stand where your feet are, for there is nowhere else to put them. Or this at least is the novice's impression—on the harder routes of the East Peak an exact one. As we mounted, the sense of the scale of Lliwedd gained on us. We felt like tiny insects creeping from ledge to ledge, from scoop to scoop, insects lost among the vertical immensities about us. All went well, the excitement of achievement blended with the radiance of the day. Crib Goch across Llydaw swam in a haze of sunlight; and when we came, after hours that had seemed like minutes, to a pleasant grassy nook that invited us to pause for rest and lunch, there could have been few happier beings in the world than we. The main difficulties were overcome. Above was easier climbing at a gentle angle. We seemed to have done what we had set out to do.

When we had eaten and smoked we went on. I had become an avid reader of the famous Climbers' Club Pocket Guide-books to the Welsh Crags, and phrases from that master of terse description, Archer Thompson, were always echoing in my memory. One of them about "belaying the rope around a stook of bollards" wandered from nowhere into my mind just then. It was well that it did so. Herbert was cautiously mounting a steep rib built of massive blocks. A tempting bollard adorned my ledge and acting more in the spirit of Thompson's phrase than from any particular apprehension I had cast a turn of the rope around it. Herbert was to my right and about fifteen feet above me.

Just as he clasped the crest of a block with both arms—somewhat in the monkey-up-a-stick position—the block yielded and heaved out with him clinging to it. How he managed to disengage himself from it I hardly saw. The physical sensation of horror, a quick but heavy pulse of sickness, flashes through one almost before one sees what is happening. Then, as though all feeling had been plucked away, a clear mental calmness follows. I had time to cry "My God! Look out!" before the block thundered down the cliff with Herbert after it. He hit my ledge and rebounded outwards, disappearing backwards from my view over the edge. Though I held him, the rope ran a little through my hands, leaving a white burn-scar that lingered on my palms for weeks. Quickly though these things happen, they seem in passing to be almost leisurely. One has time to take in the rope, time to think whether there is anything more one should do, time to decide that there is nothing, time to reflect that if the *belay* holds all will be well, and that if not . . . time to perceive with complete and vivid particularity the whole scene—the greenness of the grass ledge, the shape of the lurching boulder and the movement of the falling man, the play and course of the rope cutting into the turfy edge. Time for all this and for a pause of anguished expectancy in which to wonder just how bad what has happened will turn out to be. The pause was broken by a small voice that seemed to come from very far away saying, "I'm all right."

He was not all right by any means. Somehow with some pulling he managed to get up to my ledge, white and shaking but composed and self-possessed. Then we could see what the damage was. One leg was broken, the shin-bone being exposed for five inches. Fortunately the bleeding was slight. What proved worse was a bad sprain to the ankle. For a while he rested on the ledge. We had no brandy flask and an orange was the best I could provide as a restorative. The sleeves of the white blouse I used to sport in those early days came in usefully as bandages.

But the time came when our further movements had to be planned and undertaken. With great courage and resolution, Herbert insisted on leading up the remaining four hundred feet. He thought my climbing experience still too little to deal with such loose terrain. We were more than half-way up the cliff, no one within sight or hearing. Fortunately the day was long. The leg was less painful on the way up the cliff where it could be dragged than on the way down the endless slopes into Cwm-y-Llan. I can recall all the struggle, the coming out into the sunlight at the summit—Snowdon in a dreamy distance above us—the agonizing progress down into the Cwm, Herbert using me as a crutch. After a long while we reached a stream where we bathed the leg and I went on to telephone to a doctor and fetch a car. I recall all this and going up again at dusk to fetch him in, and then a blank of oblivion falls.

In the eyes of those not infected with mountain madness this episode should have put a proper and summary end to my climbing aspirations. And, in fact, strong parental and other influences were marshalled to prohibit them. I was forbidden to climb again. Beddgelert shook its head. The lack of all proper perspective shown in such climbing enthusiasm was pointed out to me. But in vain! After his six weeks in splints my climbing partner and I, with keenness unabated, were at it again. Even before Herbert was on his crutches, I was out on the rocks with his father. And each evening I would look in to cheer the invalid with stories of the day's doings and he, in imagination, would be sharing the climbs. The instant he was well enough, such was his ardour, he would come out to shout ribald comments to us from the Ogwen Road, as we struggled with the Milestone Buttress.

The transition now followed that is almost as palpable and decisive as the larval-imago change. Before, I had been a tourist and a walker; afterwards I at least *felt* a mountaineer. I suspect all climbers have a secret, cherished history of this phase of their development. With the change came a youthful intolerance of parties that set off to picnic with hampers, plates, knives and forks, heavy bottles of ginger-beer, tea-kettles, knitting and magazines—all the impedimenta that

root us to one spot. They seemed to bring with them all the common-
places of everyday life and spread a blight of sacrilege on the scene.
Such comforts seemed to anaesthetize one. To go up to Idwal on high-
heels in mackintoshes seemed an outrage. Rocks from above should
have been hurled by an infuriated mountain spirit on those so out of
place. I broke away with two other girls and we went up the Devil's
Kitchen track to look down into its horrific recesses. My eye of a
budding mountaineer, be it noted, had spotted a walking-route down
the true left of the Kitchen, on a grassy ledge somewhere near the
Hanging-Garden Gully! But I had mistaken the scale; what looked
like a step was a fifty-foot drop; and, when we got to its edge, panic
broke out in our party. Once we had looked over the drop, the moral
effort required to get us up the grass we had cheerfully slid down was
no slight one. This was quite a good lesson in itself and I was chas-
tened by the episode.

Little by little better judgment came and with it the collective
opposition lost its power. Solitary wanderings with map and compass
across the hills gave confidence—in more than merely technical matters. To lie on the summit of Moel Hebog alone with aneroid, compass
and map and successfully identify all the mountains in sight, was
better than being given the freedom of any city. Before, it had been
possible to spend months in Beddgelert without dreaming of going up
any of the mountains. They were unreal distant places, too far, too
tiring, pathless and dangerous in mist. Now space seemed to unfold
itself in great waves before me. To find the top of the Bristly Ridge of
Glyder Fach in mist, at dusk, alone, and come down it, was an adventure that nothing in later mountaineering could surpass. The curlews
wailing over the swamps, sheep coughing invisibly out of the greyness
on the chilly flats, the pinnacles of the ridge looming enormous and
the wind whistling through the broken wall on Bwlch Tryfan were
impressions that stamped themselves deeper than the memory. They
were patents to the faculties, licences to the imagination and the will.

«This exercise of proper judgment»
Miriam O'Brien and the Cordée Féminine, *1929*

Miriam O'Brien was born and grew up in New England. At the age of two she is said to have possessed both an independent sense of gender and a propensity for climbing: "One thing is sure," her mother wrote in an 1899 letter to a relative, "she doesn't want dolls for her birthday. I got one downtown and she turned away in disgust. Aunt Ellen came last night. She says she is going to buy her a greased pole or a tree to climb or something of that order." In 1914, when she was sixteen years old, O'Brien and her mother visited Chamonix in the French Alps, and together they went up to the Brevent, which today is reached by *telephérique* but then was accessible only by a strenuous scramble. She was suitably impressed by the view of Mont Blanc and the jagged Chamonix *aiguilles*, but had no inkling that she would someday climb so many of them.

O'Brien made her first roped climb in 1920 in the Alps. In 1925, traveling with her family through western North America, she climbed Mount Rainier, Longs Peak, and several other peaks in the Canadian Rockies—climbs that may have been significant in allowing her to gain experience without the assistance of overly solicitous Alpine guides. Even more significant was the trip she made to Mount Washington in the winter of 1925. When her brother and a companion failed to return on time from their planned ascent of the peak, O'Brien and two others, having just returned from their own climb, set out to look for them; O'Brien wound up leaving the other two searchers behind and climbing on alone through the snow. The missing climbers came in on their own quite safe, and everyone was reunited at their shelter around two o'clock that night. It was hardly a "rescue" at all, but for O'Brien the experience was formative:

> From it I learned that the sensation of fatigue may be very mislead-ing; that one has enormous unsuspected reserves of strength and endurance. What had happened? Tom and I had got back to the inn at night, after a long and exhausting day in the mountains, break-ing trail through that exceptionally heavy snow, done in, unable, we should have said, to take another step. After a short rest we had started out again [for the "rescue"] and on this second trip the incentive to keep going—and fast—had been so strong that I had not noticed any fatigue at all! After this eye-opening experience I adopted the belief that for practical purposes there was no limit to physical endurance. This may have been intellectually untenable, but for the years of my youth it seemed to do well enough as a working hypothesis. I have been, in my lifetime, extremely tired more than once. I have been too tired to eat, too tired to sleep. But I don't remember any occasion when I couldn't have walked an-other mile if my life had depended on it.

Such experiences helped prepare O'Brien for the spectacular *cordée féminine* ascents that were to make her famous in the climbing world. In the account below, excerpted from her auto-biography, *Give Me the Hills*, O'Brien first explains why she felt women had to climb without men if they wished to experience the full challenge of the sport, and then describes her most no-torious climb, that of the famous *aiguille*, the Grépon.

VERY EARLY I realized that the person who invariably climbs behind a good leader, guide or amateur, may never really learn mountaineering at all and in any case enjoys only a part of all the varied delights and rewards of climbing. He has, of course, the glorious mountain scenery, the exhilaration of physical acrobatics, the pleasure that comes from the exercise of skill, and these acrobatics often require skill to a consid-erable degree. But he is, after all, only following.

The one who goes up first on the rope has even more fun, as he solves the immediate problems of technique, tactics and strategy as they occur. And if he is, as he usually is, also the leader, the one who carries the responsibility for the expedition, he tastes the supreme joys. For mountaineering is a sport which has a considerable intellectual component. It takes judgment to supply the ideas, to make wise and proper decisions on the route, the weather, the possibility of danger from stonefall, avalanche, concealed crevasse, etc., and above all, to know what one's own capabilities permit. This exercise of proper judgment is of more consequence than in most sports, for mountaineering (like lion-hunting or white-water canoeing!) is a game with a real and sometimes drastic penalty for failure. You don't have merely to pretend that it is important to play the game well.

I saw no reason why women, *ipso facto*, should be incapable of leading a good climb. They had, as a matter of fact, already done so, on some few scattered occasions. But why not make it a regular thing, on the usual climbs of the day? Henry de Ségnogne went to some pains to explain to me why a woman could never lead a climb. There is a lot more to leading, said Henry, than first meets the eye, a lot that must be learned, and that is best learned by watching competent leaders attentively and coming to understand their decisions. Women, however, never bother to do this. Since they know that they will never be allowed to lead anyway, they just come walking along behind, looking at the scenery. Therefore, even if they were given an opportunity to lead, they would be completely unprepared. I didn't find this argument too convincing, but I did realize that if women were really to lead, that is, to take the entire responsibility for the climb, there couldn't be any man at all in the party. For back in the 1920's women were perhaps a bit more sheltered than they are today. And in any emergency, particularly in an outdoor sport like mountaineering, what man wouldn't spring to the front and take over? I decided to try some climbs not only guideless but manless.

The first step along this path was to learn to lead the rope, with a competent man behind. Early in 1927 in the Dolomites I had done a little leading where the going was pretty easy, although it did worry dear old Antonio almost intolerably. With Angelo I could lead all I liked, just so long as we were out of sight of his father, but the places I went with Angelo were almost invariably too difficult for me to go up without the security of a rope from above. For it does make a difference! You need a much greater margin of safety when you are leading; with a rope from above that would hold you if things got too tough for your ability, you can launch out on pitches much nearer your limit. Later in the summer of 1927 I laid plans to lead the Grépon at Chamonix and my guide Alfred Couttet agreed to come along as second man. I took this decision late in the season and the weather was never favourable for the attempt. The next year, however, I did lead the Grépon, taking with me the porter Georges Cachat.

The Grépon now, in these days of improved technique and equipment and thereby higher standards of difficulty, does not count for so much as it used to. Even in those days many longer and much harder climbs had been done. But it was at that time among the most renowned of the Chamonix Aiguilles, having for many past years enjoyed the reputation of being one of the finest rock-climbs in the Alps, and it was still a climb that not all the licensed Chamonix guides could lead. On September 8, 1928, Georges Cachat and I traversed the Grépon with me in the lead. Everything went well. Although not attempting to hurry, we were on the summit a little after 10 and back at the Montenvers at 1.15—good average time for a competent party. That was on a Saturday. Early Sunday morning, asleep in my bed at the Hotel des Alpes in Chamonix, I was awakened by a congratulatory cablegram from my mother back home in Dedham, Massachusetts. Black Magic! I could think of no other way she could have learned about this. It developed however that Black Magic had been helped out by the machinations of the Associated Press.

But I still wanted to do the Grépon really manless.

The next summer, having found out that leading was simpler than it had looked from a distance, I turned to real manless climbing. In spite of Dean Peabody's later observations that it must have been hard to find a woman who was "strong physically and weak mentally," I had many women friends who were excellent climbers and I was able to persuade some of them to go with me.

My first manless climb was an ascent of the Aiguille du Peigne with Winifred Marples on August 14, 1929. The Peigne, shorter and easier than the Grépon, still presents the same type of climbing up its bold, precipitous walls of good, firm Chamonix granite. We spent the night before our climb at the little châlet of Plan de l'Aiguille, just under the Peigne. That evening we walked out a little to look over the route we should have to take the next morning, while it was still dark, up across the grassy alplands and grassy moraines, towards the peak. That's something you never worry about when you go with a guide, but before each manless climb I always scouted the start of the route. It would be entirely possible, and embarrassing, I think, to get lost leaving the hut.

The ascent of the Peigne went off well, and three days later, August 17, Alice Damesme and I made the first manless traverse of the Grépon. Starting from the Montenvers at 2.35 A.M., in three hours we had reached the Rognon des Nantillons, a rocky promontory emerging from the lower end of the Glacier des Nantillons. This was the standard breakfast spot and here we joined several other caravans bound for the various peaks above. Naturally, on an occasion like this, everyone chats a bit about their various projects and when, under questioning, it developed that Alice and I planned to do the Grépon it caused some commotion.

"Vous deux seules?" [Just the two of you?] was the incredulous exclamation.

They were too courteous to laugh at us outright, but we did intercept quite a lot of sideways glances and barely-concealed smiles. Alice and I pretended not to notice. Breakfast over, the other parties all held back and allowed us to lead off up the glacier and over the bergschrund to the rocks below the Charmoz-Grépon Col, that depression between the Charmoz to the north and the Grépon to the south. The present-day route varies in some minor points, but we followed of course the route of 1929. The weather was none too good, with a lot of clouds and mist. Still, the only party actually coming down was Bradford Washburn's movie crew, who had decided that there would be no sun for pictures that day.

The bergschrund really did give us quite a lot of trouble but we couldn't waste much time on it with that large and rapidly-growing audience below. Finally we crossed under a big boulder and then squirmed up a steep narrow crack between the boulder and the ice, clawing away with our axes for holds on the outside of the ice wall. Above the bergschrund we started up easy, half-familiar rocks but soon we felt sure we were going much too far to the left. There was mist all around us and we could see very little. The routes to the Charmoz and the Grépon diverged about here and we might well be on our way to the Charmoz. We wouldn't have asked directions of any of those men in the world! We were playing a game and we must abide by the rules: no help from men! With a few rapid, surreptitious whispers we took our decision: we would go right ahead with feigned assurance, and if we later found ourselves on the Charmoz we would traverse both peaks and pretend that was what we had meant to do all along. (I believe we might have done it, too!) But later we found a way to edge over to the right and get near the proper couloir. It was not the usual route. As we approached the col, still on the north bank of the couloir, the rocks were steep, icy and loose. When the porter Alfred Burnet, who was already at the col, first saw us through the mist, he excitedly shouted that he would throw us down a rope. We declined with thanks this superfluous rescue.

As we got still nearer the col along came Armand Charlet with Guido Alberto Rivetti of Biella, Italy, whom we met there for the first time. They had come over the Charmoz, bound for the Grépon, and we took it for granted, since they had reached the col first, that they would go right along up the Grépon ahead of us. We were a little disappointed since we had hoped to be the first to climb the Mummery Crack. Perhaps Armand realized this, and it reinforced his decision.

"We will have lunch here, Monsieur," said he, casually, as he sat down.

Guido Rivetti looked astounded, as well he might. It was no time for lunch, and hardly a suitable place for it, either. And such a suggestion to come from that speed demon Armand! But he caught on at once: something was about to happen here that Armand wanted to watch.

The summit ridge of the Grépon, as almost every mountain climber knows, resembles a crenelated wall, approximately horizontal, with five or six great spires or pinnacles. The traverse of the Grépon consists in reaching this ridge at its north end and climbing over and around the pinnacles to the south, where one descends to the Col des Nantillons. On the west side the sheer granite wall drops in one sweep 1,500 feet to the upper reaches of the Glacier des Nantillons; on the east, nearly 5,000 feet to the Mer de Glace. To attain the ridge in the first place, from the Charmoz-Grépon Col, it is necessary to tackle what was one of the most famous climbing problems of the day, the Mummery Crack. The wall of the Grépon rising above the col is unbroken except for a narrow crack between the main wall of granite and a half-detached slab that lies against it, the Mummery Crack. It does not lead directly from the col, but starts somewhat off to the side, above the precipice to the west. This narrow crack is climbed by a caterpillar motion. You jam in the right hand and the right foot, and raise them alternately, first supporting your weight on your foot and working your hand higher, then holding everything on your jammed fist and again wedging the foot a little above. The left hand feels over the outside of the slab clinging, as Mummery said of another of his climbs, "to slight discolorations in the rock." There is not much for the left foot to do. All this takes place pretty far up in the air. Not only is the crack itself sixty feet high, but there is nothing below its base to break the view for another thousand feet. The second man, assuring the rope from a little notch just above the col at the side, would not be of much use if you once started bounding down the cliffs below the crack. Climbers have fallen out of the Mummery Crack but no leader has ever fallen from near the top of it and lived! The ascent of this crack is easier if you stay well outside and insert your hand and foot just a short distance. But the exposure is so great that there is an unconscious urge to jam yourself inside the crack as far as possible. This leads to tense and rigid muscles and is the shortest route to getting stuck and having a serious struggle. The key to an easy ascent of the Mummery Crack is complete relaxation.

Alice and I changed our boots for light climbing shoes. There was no question of who should lead: I had already had that pleasure; it was Alice's turn. When I was firmly installed at the little notch above the col where the second man does what he can to belay the rope for the leader, Alice started off in a matter-of-fact way although there was around us an atmosphere of some tenseness and excitement. Nowadays climbers, starting from the col, reach the midpoint of the crack by a traverse on small holds and a couple of pitons, but then it was the custom, at least for the leader, to climb the whole crack from the bottom. To reach this base of the crack it was necessary to descend 45–50 feet from the notch. The rocks in the couloir here were icy and loose, and Alice dislodged quite a sizeable one. Considering that several parties were already congregated at the col, we were surprised to hear a vehement outcry from two more still in the couloir below, as they heard this rock bounding down towards them. They successfully took shelter.

"Are you up the Mummery crack?" shouted Maurice Damesme, Alice's husband, who was traversing the Charmoz that day with Winifred Marples and Réné Picard, and who could not see us for the mist.

"Almost," cheerfully replied Alice, who had not yet reached its base.

At the bottom of the crack Alice left her rucksack and started up. The take-off is a difficult pitch, not vertical but overhanging for about the first eight to ten feet, so that Alice was leaning backwards as she tried to pull herself up the smooth rock. She did not get it instantaneously, but soon she did, and was climbing upward smoothly and confidently. It was, as might have been expected, the performance of a real expert.

"Dîtes donc!" [So tell us] shouted the boys from below in the couloir. "Is it safe to come out now?"

Alice stopped short just where she was and called down to them the most ardent apologies.

"Toutes mes excuses. . . ." [My apologies.]

This indeed testified to a poise and sangfroid quite out of the ordinary!

The boys poked their heads out from behind their rock and I was immensely amused to watch the expressions on their faces when they saw where Alice was, and that there was no one above her. In reply to her apologies they stumblingly assured her that it was indeed a pleasure and an honour to have rocks knocked on you by a lady who . . . Still, they couldn't quite believe it.

About this time it occurred to me that even though the day was cloudy I should like to have a picture; my camera, however, was some six feet away. Alice offered to wait until I got it. Never mind, Armand was bringing it to me. As I accepted the camera from him I realized that this was our first deviation from the manless principle!

Midway up the crack an outward-sloping shelf affords a welcome rest. From there on, although the crack is somewhat wider and the angle eases off a little from the vertical, still this second thirty feet continues to be laborious and fatiguing, particularly for the climber who has climbed the entire sixty feet. When Alice reached the top, the watching crowd broke into enthusiastic and well-deserved cheers.

Then in my turn I went down the couloir to the base of the crack, and for the first time realized that our two rucksacks should have been pulled up from the notch on the side, and not all the way from the bottom. It was no easy job for Alice to haul these things up sixty feet with our nailed boots and other heavy gear inside.

When I had led the Mummery Crack the preceding year it had seemed to me surprisingly easy and I was astonished this time to find it had once again become much more laborious. There is indubitably a stimulation to going up first, it seems to me; the excitement and elation bring on a real increase in strength and skill.

The usual custom for a guided party then was to have the tourist swing across on the rope to the middle platform, but today Armand refused to allow Guido Rivetti to do this.

"Today, Monsieur," he suggested, "I don't think that today, since two ladies have climbed the crack from the bottom, it would be appropriate for a man to take an easier route. Would it not be better if you started where they did?"

"But naturally. Of course," Guido Rivetti replied, shaking with laughter as he made his way down the couloir to the takeoff. Some climbers could easily have been inconvenienced by this, but since

Guido Rivetti was one of Italy's foremost alpinists and had made many difficult climbs guideless, he was more entertained than discommoded.

From the top of the crack Alice and I called to Maurice to reassure him and started on, with me ahead for the moment, up through the Trou du Canon and out on to the Mer de Glace face. After a little traverse there is a short chimney with an overhanging block closing in the top, a tricky pitch, although of course not long. I remember how uneasy Georges had been the year before when I had gone up here. A few snowflakes had drifted down as I was climbing the Mummery Crack and now we were caught in a brief but severe blizzard of snow, with a high wind and extreme cold. We stopped in a sheltered place to put on our sweaters and mittens. We should really have changed to our nailed boots again too, but for the moment it seemed just too cold to do so, and we kept on as we were.

Then came the other famous pitches on the Grépon, the Boîte aux Lettres, that narrow crack where you wriggle through sideways with the crack going on down indefinitely below you, the Rateau de Chèvre, and the Grand Gendarme. To get off this Grand Gendarme to the notch on the farther side, a descent of fifty sheer unclimbable feet, you rope off—but not in the usual way, straight down as the rope hangs, which would land you not at the notch at all but somewhere out on the Mer de Glace face. Instead, laying the mid-point of the rope over a little projection, you then slide down the sharp vertical edge of the summit block à cheval, holding one strand of the rope out on the left wall and one on the right. The start is sensational, backing off into space with a drop below of more than a thousand feet. I have seen big, strong men (but, to be honest, men inexperienced in climbing) hesitate before getting up their courage to do this even though they were held firmly on a second rope by a guide above. Alice and I were not held by any second rope. Being too lazy to carry two ropes, we were climbing on my 150-foot alpine line. When we needed it for roping down, as here, we took it off our waists.

The actual summit of the Grépon is a large flat rock. The Rivetti-Charlet party had passed us on the traverse but here we four met again and had lunch together, watched (since the snow flurry had stopped) through the telescope in Chamonix by my mother and Christiane, Alice's little girl. (Christiane today will not permit her children to do any mountain climbing with Grandma and Grandpa, but will allow a little skiing!) It was a gay lunch, enlivened by an impassioned oration, no less, by Guido Rivetti on the humiliation suffered by a man, and a man who had considered himself a good climber, at being escorted over the Grépon by a guide on a day such as this.

To leave the summit of the Grépon you rope off on the Mer de Glace side, where the drop to the glacier below is a vertical mile. Armand had already placed his *corde de rappel*, which he invited us to use. Just casting to the winds all our scruples about taking aid from men, we accepted. As Alice was roping down and I was belaying her, I saw Armand's hand shoot out a time or two to grasp her rope. He thought in time and did not touch it, but his desire to do so was almost irresistible. From the Col des Nantillons we went down the glacier in the usual way to the Rognon, where we met Maurice, Winifred and Réné.

"The Grépon has disappeared," said Etienne Bruhl, sadly, that evening in Chamonix. "Of course," he admitted, "there are still some rocks standing there, but as a climb it no longer exists. Now that it has been done by two women alone, no self-respecting man can undertake it. A pity, too, because it used to be a very good climb."

A. F. Mummery, that superlative climber who made the first ascent of the Grépon in 1881, wrote: "It has frequently been noticed that all mountains appear doomed to pass through the three stages: an inaccessible peak—the most difficult ascent in the Alps—an easy day for a lady." He went on to say: "I must confess that the Grépon has not yet reached this final stage, and the heading . . . must be regarded as prophetic rather than as a statement of actual fact."

«Alone at Last»

Nea Morin Climbs the Meije and the Blaitière, 1933

Nea Morin, after Loulou Boulaz perhaps the best woman
climber active in the interwar years, was born Nea Barnard in
1906 in England. Hers was a climbing family: her father was a
member of the Alpine Club, her brothers were all active
climbers, and even the family doctor had once been the Alpine
Club president. She made her first roped climbs when she was
sixteen; three years later she made a guideless ascent of the
10,650-foot Diableret, which proved an early test of her route-
finding skills. The next year, she and her friend Winifred Marples made a trip to Chamonix, where she met Jean Morin, her
future husband, who was already a well-known climber and a
founder of what then was perhaps the most exclusive mountaineering club in the world—the Groupe de Haute Montagne,
or GHM, open only to alpinists who had demonstrated an ability to lead the most difficult climbs without guides.

Nea climbed extensively with Jean but also had a network
of skilled woman partners, including Marples, Jean's sister Micheline Morin, and Alice Damesme, whom she had met while
training at the Fountainebleau boulders near Paris. The women
enjoyed climbing *en cordée féminine*, though after Nea's marriage, the husbands in her climbing circle became increasingly
solicitous for the safety of the wives, a situation which apparently changed little even when she was admitted to the elite
GHM. The account below, excerpted from Morin's autobiography *A Woman's Reach*, reveals how difficult it remained for even
the most skilled women to slip away for a climb that would be
truly their own.

IT IS CLAIMED for the Meije that it is the most difficult of the major Alpine peaks to attain. The easiest way up the Grand Pic is quite hard and was not climbed until 1877—twelve years after the Matterhorn and the Aiguille Verte—by M. Boileau de Castelnau with Pierre Gaspard *père et fils*. The traverse of the arêtes from the Pic Central or Doigt de Dieu, to the Grand Pic was not done until 1885 by Emil and Otto Zsigmondy and Ludwig Purtscheller; the traverse in the opposite direction—the present normal route—not until 1891.

By some miscalculation of the powers that be the Meije just fails to attain the magic 4,000 metre mark. To be numbered among the great company of four-thousanders a peak must be 13,123 feet, and the Meije falls short of this by just 42 feet. Nevertheless it is a formidable as well as a strikingly beautiful peak. In early times Meije was often written Meidje, the "d" being a left-over from the old appellation l'Oeuille dou Meid-jour—l'Aiguille du Milieu du Jour—just another Aiguille du Midi.

Owing to its position this mountain attracts a great deal of bad weather and few are those who succeed at the first attempt in making the traverse—up the Grand Muraille, over the Grand Pic, down into the sombre Brèche Zsigmondy, along the airy crests of the three rocky Dents, then the Dent de Neige and the Doigt de Dieu, and finally down the icy north slopes to the Refuge de l'Aigle, and by the long, long Côte Longue to La Grave.

In 1925 the Meije had repulsed me, but in 1933 Alice, Micheline and I had plans for a traverse *en cordée féminine*.

The rendezvous of our group of G.H.M. friends was the Pré de Madame Carle, above Ailefroide, which at this time was still idyllic. The road stopped short of the rushing torrent of St. Pierre; aptly named, for the bridge was not suitable for cars, and so a paradise it blessedly remained. We humped our camping gear along just beyond the Club Alpin Français Refuge Cézanne, which was so primitive that it attracted few visitors. Nearby was a small stone house where lived Adeline Rodier, widow of one of the numerous Rodiers of La Bérarde. She was the *gardienne* of the hut and gave us our *café au lait* in the mornings, and often our evening meal as well, set on a long trestle table out of doors. She became a very dear friend to us all, but more particularly to Jean and the two Vernet brothers who so loved this secluded corner of the Dauphiné Alps.

The torrents coming from the Glacier Blanc and the Glacier Noir fan out in a wide delta over the Pré de Madame Carle, and the water warms up as it runs shallowly over hot white stones under a blazing

Left to right: Micheline Morin, Nea Morin, and Alice Damesme at the Aigle hut following the first *cordée féminine* traverse of the Meije in 1933.

sun, providing a ready-made bathing establishment. Still in bathing dresses we would toboggan down the névés near at hand, névés that have now followed the trend of the retreating glaciers and withdrawn far above.

But now came news of tragedy. Paris, a member of the G.H.M., had been killed on the Pelvoux. He had fallen in a place that was extremely difficult and dangerous to get to, and the guides, not surprisingly, did not want to risk their lives for a dead body. However the body had to be recovered as questions of insurance were involved. All the friends went to help, but it was not until Armand Charlet arrived from Chamonix that the pathetic sack, bearing no resemblance to the form of a human body, was brought down to the Pré de Madame Carle.

But it was the beginning of our holidays, and we were full of ambitious plans. Once we had done what we could, these sad happenings had to be put firmly out of mind.

As a training trip Jean and I, with Maurice Damesme and Albert Roux went to complete the west ridge of the Montagne des Agneaux, the lower part of which Jean had already done in 1931; we now made a route joining the ridge at the spot where he and his companions had turned back, and completed it to the summit. It was a good climb and we felt elated—a success so early in the holidays was, in my experience of guideless climbing, unusual. We were descending by the ordinary route towards the Col Tuckett when we saw two stationary figures on the glacier below. Were those cries of distress? Our hearts sank as we hurried to the scene. There had been an accident all right, and such a pitiful one. One man with some experience and two beginners had been ascending a snow slope of perhaps 45 degrees. The man, who was leading, had come to a crevasse and had skirted along far too close to its upper lip while looking for a way across; the edge of the crevasse was undercut and he fell through. This might still not have resulted in tragedy but for the fact that the leader had coils of rope round his chest which he had not taken the precaution to fasten to his waist-loop. When he fell the coils must have tightened immediately; he would have lost consciousness almost at once and died in a matter of minutes. The two young fellows said they had been unable to get any reply from him after he fell in. When we arrived it was already some time after the accident and the rope had cut deeply into the edge of the crevasse. We tried in vain for several hours to extricate the body; all we could do was to fix the rope and go down to alert the guides.

This second tragedy sadly reduced our morale.

It now seemed highly doubtful whether Alice, Micheline and I would ever get Maurice and Jean to consent to our proposed *cordée féminine* on the Meije, and still more doubtful whether we ourselves would have the necessary courage. However, in the end they reluctantly agreed to our going round to La Bérarde. On the way we stopped at Les Claux, at the house of Albert Roux's parents, who entertained us in a high, cool, white-washed living-room. Sipping our drinks we exchanged news and were asked our plans. We did not say much, but enough to turn the conversation towards the Meije. "*Ah, elle en a tué des hommes*" [That peak has killed some], said our host, little thinking that his words struck an icy chill in our hearts.

We went on our way feeling far from cheerful. Jean had remained with our friends at Ailefroide. Maurice came with us as far as Bourg d'Oisans and then continued on to Grenoble, about twenty miles distant. Bourg d'Oisans is at the junction of the roads descending from La Grave in the valley of the Romanche, to the north of the Meije, with that descending from La Bérarde in the Val Vénéon, to the south of the *massif*.

Still sad at parting with Jean and Maurice we took the bus up to La
Bérarde and here we received another blow to our extremely shaky
morale. At the little Hotel Tairraz I found George Peaker, who with a
friend had just traversed the Meije from La Bérarde. After the climb
the friend had remained at the Aigle hut to wait for their rappel rope
which they had left at the last steep slopes over the rimaye for the use
of another party coming behind. Meanwhile George had gone on
down to La Grave in order to telephone his wife at La Bérarde to tell
her they had completed their climb safely. Then, without waiting for
his friend, he caught a bus back to La Bérarde. Next day when we
arrived George was beginning to worry because his friend had not
turned up. At dinner a phone call came through to say that he had
been killed. It was already late when he started down from the hut, he
missed his way, which is difficult to find, and fell to his death.

A dejected trio made its way up to the Promontoire hut next day.
We no longer had any heart for the venture. "It is an ill wind . . ." and
all of us were secretly relieved to hear it moaning round the hut that
night, presaging no good. Thankfully we tucked our heads further
under our blankets with that guilty feeling of relief well-known to all
climbers. In the morning we had to return to La Bérarde. Here we
found Maurice, unable to keep away. He told us the day on which we
had intended to traverse the Meije was an unlucky date for him. Now
that it was safely past he wanted to come along too. But what of our
cordée féminine? He replied, with reason, that if we thought we should
have the Meije to ourselves, we were much mistaken. It was not the
moment to make difficulties, and next day we again set off for the
Promontoire, this time in company with Maurice and three friends.

All went well. We had perfect weather and good conditions and
Alice, Micheline and I climbed *en cordée féminine*, dividing the lead
between us. Alice led at the Brèche Zsigmondy, the crux of the climb
and, once one has rappeled down into it from the Grand Pic, the point
of no return. Beyond is a most impressive pitch, a crack which disap-
pears round an ominous corner on the steep and nearly always ice-
coated north face. But Alice led it imperturbably. Up and down we
climbed, along that airy crest with the mountain dropping away sheer
on either side, over the Dents de Neige and the Doigt de Dieu to the
final rappel down across the rimaye, and so to the Aigle hut. We had
no food so we decided to continue down to La Grave that evening. My
last memory is of descending Côte Longue (as one did then); this is a
punishing descent at the end of a day, for the Aigle is at 11,000 feet and

La Grave at 5,000. To ease the strain on my not so good knee, I took a
zigzag course, and as I went tacking down the slope, at intervals I crossed
the direct course taken by the others. Seeing this queer frenzied figure
continually looming up out of the gloom, crossing and re-crossing their
path, going full speed ahead in order to keep up, the others merely
smiled to themselves—they had always known the English were mad.
Eventually we reached La Grave, blessed beds, and sleep.

Our next manless venture, on the Blaitière in 1934, I described at
the time in an article in the Ladies' Alpine Club Journal entitled
Ladies Only. I repeat this account here slightly edited as a period piece,
conveying our excitement at going off without husbands and brothers.

Alone at last! Alice, Micheline and I found ourselves on the
terrace of the Montenvers Hotel, having just speeded our male friends
and relatives on their way to the Requin hut, thus accomplishing by far
the most difficult and trying part of our programme.

All summer we had hoped to do a climb really on our own, but the
way of the would-be "manless" climber is fraught with many an obstacle unknown to the general mountaineering public. Several times we
had been together on a rope, but always with a party of friends near at
hand, as on the Meije the previous year, and under such conditions
more than half the sense of adventure is lost.

Now, with our holidays practically at an end, we felt desperately
that we should not have another chance; up to the last moment we let
it be understood that we would take part in a general expedition,
conditions making it impossible for us to attempt any of the climbs on
our "ladies only" list. The expedition the men proposed was to be a
biggish one and we were to be allowed to follow *en cordée féminine*, an
excellent idea from their point of view, as we could thus be kept under
surreptitious but constant observation. We on our side, they felt, would
be able, with a little timely short-sightedness, aided by a great deal of
imagination, to make believe that we were on our own. But Micheline
thought otherwise. In the morning, all assembled to discuss plans; with
a warlike glitter in her eye, Micheline blandly announced that we were
going off to do something *quite* on our own. Alice and I sat tight
waiting for the inevitable explosion, for on these occasions Micheline
was the spokesman of the party. Throughout the season Maurice had
manoeuvred successfully to keep his wife in sight, so it was little
wonder he was not pleased with this plan. Micheline had hard work to
obtain the required permission, but as a valiant and experienced man-

less climber she had all the answers. When we suggested that we might try the Blaitière, the men looked scornful. Why do a climb like that when we had the opportunity of a much better one if we followed them? No argument, however, could shake our determination. So here we were at the Montenvers, somewhat exhausted and not a little ashamed at having sent the men away so callously; but sunbathing on the grassy ledges above the hotel and tea on the terrace soon restored us. After all, the others would enjoy doing a fine trip, and once we were back from our little fugue, with their fears for our safety set at rest, they would be almost more delighted than we ourselves.

From the Col des Nantillons we surveyed the ridge of the Rocher de la Corde up which we should have to make our way. The snow-covered rocks looked black and white, cold and uninviting in the early morning light. Just as Alice reached the crest of the arête, she dropped her axe, no doubt owing to frozen fingers, and away it went clattering and banging down to the Envers de Blaitière glacier. Fortunately the loss of an axe would hinder us very little if at all, but we felt it was far more important that we did not have to face scornful males.

The day was cloudless, the sun already beginning to thaw our fingers and it was a joy to pause for a deep breath and a glance down to the sparkling glaciers or up to the surrounding Aiguilles.

We overflowed with content and good humour: this was, after all, the beginning of the only fine day any of us experienced on the mountains that summer. No need to hurry, no need to force ourselves to the limit before making the longed-for halt. Time to take photos, to rest, to eat.

A short rappel down the smooth wall of the Rocher de la Corde, so called because of the fixed rope left there, and we found ourselves on the heels of the guided party. They seemed surprised to see us, and still more surprised when we politely declined their good-natured offer of a rope up the next pitch, and in consequence had to try to look as professional and dignified as possible while giving the leader a shoulder up. We were touched by the fatherly eye kept on us by the guides; more than once they offered us aid or tips as to what to do, though of course with the condescending masculine amuse-yourselves-as-much-as-you-like-and-we-are-always-at-hand-to-come-to-the-rescue smile.

We basked in the sun eating oranges, while making a short halt to allow the guided party to get ahead again. They went straight for the Pointe Centrale, much to our joy, since we intended climbing the

Pointe de Chamonix first. Leaving all but one small sack behind we set off with lightened steps up the sharp snow arête and across the top of the Spencer couloir to the *demi-lune*. Alice did not seem to notice the loss of her axe, but then she is one of those people who are always at ease in the mountains, whatever the circumstances. We raced up the easy rocks of the Pointe de Chamonix, just stopping a few minutes on the summit to take photos and give a view-halloo to the others now on the Pointe Centrale. Then down again and back across the *demi-lune* before the sun had had time to efface our steps.

At the Montenvers we met friends nearly all returning from successful trips, but no husbands or brother. A few minutes before the last train to Chamonix, Maurice turned up bathed in perspiration and ready to be furious had we not been there. He had raced down from the Requin Hut, in something less than half the usual time, saying to himself, "If they do the three peaks they are sure to miss the last train, and then won't I scold them!" I think he was almost disappointed to find us washed and brushed and cool, comfortably installed drinking tea with our friends.

We hustled into the train down to Chamonix, a joyous group although, for most of us, it was the last trip of the season.

We three were very pleased with ourselves, perhaps even more so than after our traverse of the Meije. Fortunately we did not share the opinion of a friend who, when he saw Micheline's list of climbs for 1934, remarked scornfully, "If conditions don't allow one to do anything better than Blaitière, one stays in Chamonix." We enjoyed ourselves more than on many a technically finer climb, no doubt because there were no men friends at hand.

«I was the one on trial»
Gwen Moffat's First Season as a Professional Guide, 1953

Following the Second World War, a new sort of climber appeared in Britain. In many ways the antithesis of the well-to-do mountaineer who had been the norm and for whom climbing was a genteel pastime, the new breed was young, typically working-class, only sporadically employed and often, especially in the years after the war, hard up for cash. Unable to afford regular visits abroad, they created their climbing challenges at home, on the crags and cliffs of the British countryside, continually upping the ante by seeking out the steepest and most difficult lines of ascent, sometimes spending days to work out a route on a cliff only a hundred feet high and finding in sheer gymnastic intensity challenges comparable to those presented by much longer climbs in the Alps.

In reference to both their difficult lives and the extreme difficulty of the rock climbs they pioneered, the men who excelled at this new game were called "hard men." But the new breed was not exclusively male: Gwen Moffat, born in Brighton in 1924, led a life as hard as any and became one of the leading climbers of the 1950s. During the war, fresh out of school and with few prospects, she entered the military but disliked it intensely. In 1946, after falling in with a group of conscientious objectors and making her first rock climbs on the cliffs of Wales, she deserted and set out on a journey across Britain, passing her nights in barns and abandoned cottages and her days walking and hitchhiking northward with Thomas, a dog she befriended along the roadside. She had no particular destination, and spent

months on the road before returning to Wales to turn herself in
to a military policewoman.

After serving her desertion sentence Moffat was discharged.
By this time she was, she wrote later, "completely converted to
climbing," and she managed to live on her lump-sum separation
pay for six months, climbing at every opportunity. When the
money ran out she picked up jobs here and there and continued
climbing regularly. By 1949, she was married and had a daughter, Sheena, but was hardly leading a settled life. She and her
husband lived on an abandoned boat they had found and restored, and neither of them had a steady job. The marriage
soon fell apart. Moffat tried supporting herself by writing and
managed to sell an occasional script, but it was not until 1953,
when she earned a Guide's Certificate from the British Mountaineering Council, that she was able to have a steady income
without sacrificing the sport she loved.

Moffat still found it a less than ideal life. She regretted, for
example, having to place Sheena in a boarding school while she
worked, and the pay could be considered good only in compari-
son to the poverty she had known before. But guiding and in-
structing generally kept her in good form for her own climbing
holidays. She began writing again—today her published works
run to several crime novels and three autobiographical climbing
books—and also remarried (her second husband, Johnnie Lees, is
the "Johnnie" mentioned in the excerpt below). Her climbing
books were well received, praised for making accessible to the un-
initiated the strangely compelling attractions of the sport and for
the vividly revealed humanity of their author.

Most of Moffat's clients and students were men. Unlike the
women climbers who had preceded her, Moffat faced the challenge not only of proving her ability to doubting males but also
of justifying her authority over them. In the account below,
reprinted from her first book, *Space Below My Feet,* Moffat
describes how she did both at the outset of her professional
career—and also gives a glimpse of what was surely a hard and
a beautiful life.

I LEFT FORT WILLIAM in April and spent the Easter holidays with
Sheena in Sussex. I was very relieved to hear her talk about her new

Gwen Moffat on the English Lake District's Milestone Superdirect
route, which she climbed in 1952 with Denise Morin. Photographer:
S. R. G. Bray. Photo courtesy of the Pinnacle Club.

school with obvious enjoyment. Life became less complicated. All I had to do now was make enough money to pay school fees three times a year. These seemed exorbitant, but I had the comforting thought that if anything happened to me—such as temporary illness or unemployment—she was happy and safe. By the time I was on the road north again, heading for Langdale, I was feeling, if not exactly confident, at least a little aggressive towards the Enemy watching for that first slip.

I hitched north. I couldn't afford to go by train because my salary included expenses and I must keep these to a minimum. By nightfall that first evening I had reached Windermere. The last bus had left for Ambleside so I walked down to the shore and found a patch of grass where I could lie and listen to the ripples a few feet away. It was a clear, starlit night with no wind. After a while I became aware of something moving in the bushes.

I stared at the dark tangle of brambles until my eyes ached, wondering when this nasty man (who had, obviously, been very close when I undressed) would leap out on me. But the rustling continued and no-one came. Reluctantly, I crawled out of the bag and crept across the grass to the bushes. In the light of my torch I found a hedge-hog grubbing for worms.

I lay on my back and stared at the stars and remembered another night, years ago, when I came to an old straw stack on the Cornish cliffs, and thought a tramp had staked his claim before me, for the straw rustled without visible agency, and closer inspection showed that it *moved*. It was full of rats. I had been too tired to move on, so I pulled the drawstring of my sleeping bag over my head, and hoped they wouldn't eat their way through the down. They left me alone, but ate a neat hole in my rucksack and left nothing of my food but crumbs.

Langdale was basking in spring sunshine when I arrived the following morning. The first course was not due to start for another week, and my object in coming early was to familiarise myself with the easier climbs in the district. I pitched my tent in a field full of new lambs and celandines and went out to look for a climbing partner.

At the end of the week I met my first course. They were four young men all of whom had had previous experience of rock climbing. I tried to appear cool and business-like, but now that I was confronted with the situation after weeks of brooding over it, there was an element of hysteria in my welcome. Despite the fact that I had to pass or fail them at the end of a fortnight, I was the one on trial.

On that first morning I took them up Middlefell Buttress: five of us, all on one rope. It was slow, cold and boring. They climbed faster than I did, surrounded with an almost visible aura of masculine resentment. So I took them to Gwynne's Chimney on Pavey Ark, and as they struggled and sweated in that smooth cleft, with sparks flying from their nails, and me waiting at the top with a taut rope and a turn round my waist, I knew that I had won. The atmosphere—when we were all together again—was clean and relaxed. They could look me in the eye and say,

"Have we got any more like that? I thought it was going to be easy when you went up it . . ."

And I could laugh and say, "You'll be leading it by the end of the week."

I was no longer a woman with a reputation, but an instructor with a technique superior to theirs, and now we could settle down to work.

I took them to Bowfell Buttress—not five on a rope this time, but in two parties. The great difficulty of these courses was that there was only one leader: myself. When Johnnie ran Mountain Rescue courses with pupils who were more experienced generally than mine, he never had more than two novices to one instructor. I might, after the first week of an Intermediate course, weed out another leader, perhaps two, who could take the strong seconds up a Difficult, even a Very Difficult, but I was always very wary of letting people lead, and the parties kept close, on parallel climbs, with myself tense and watchful and almost unaware of my own climb, all eyes for the other two leaders.

During the first few days, however, I was extremely cautious, with the result that the students received only half the rock climbing I thought they should have. When we went to Bowfell Buttress I sent two people on a walk to the summit by way of Brown Ghyll and Crinkle Crags while I took the other two straight to the cliff and climbed. We met on the top and the two who had climbed reversed the walk while I led the others up the buttress.

By the second day of the course I had recovered my sense of proportion and was astonished when I remembered my fears of the last few weeks. Certainly the work was extremely exacting, but it was, on the whole, fun. I forgot the Enemy watching for a slip and revelled in the easier classics of Langdale. The two basic moods on a climb were, first, delight while I was actually climbing—perhaps tempered a little by the necessity to tell a dreaming second to watch me and not the view—and then the sense of confidence and responsibility as my seconds followed and I approved their style and neat movements; and I saw, with amused surprise, that they had watched me carefully. Usually I had no doubt that they were better than the day before.

It was capricious weather. The day might be spent in the hotel doing theory with the rain curtains drifting down the dale, and the night clutching the tent poles as the gales came roaring down on me, shaking and snatching at the canvas, while the guy ropes strained and slackened—and the stream rose—and finally I slept from sheer exhaustion. One night mine was the only tent left standing. Even the proper mountain tents were blown away and one of the caravans behind the farm was tossed over like a doll's house.

In contrast there were hot still days on Gimmer when, at lunch time, we sunbathed at the foot of the cliff; or (the same place) in mist when Oliverson's seemed as exposed as a climb on Scafell, and another day—so hot that we were too lazy to tramp all the way to Pavey Ark, but turned aside and, in shirt sleeves and plimsolls, ran up and down all the little routes on Tarn Crag.

The heat wave continued. My engagement ended and Mr. Bellamy drove me south to Glencoe where I was due to climb with Monica Jackson. And how we climbed! Not hard stuff, nothing more than Very Difficult, but we took full advantage of that glorious weather, out early in the morning and coming home in the dusk.

The first climb was Crowberry Ridge. Then I wanted to do something new, and what appealed to me most was that great west face of the Aonach Dubh which is such an obvious feature of Glencoe as seen from Ballachulish ferry: an elephant-grey wall supported by powerful buttresses and seamed with gullies. Monica was in favour of this face— in that good weather no day could go wrong—and I think she felt, too, that this formidable wall would repay exploration.

We set off early one morning from Achtriochtan, watched with disapproval by an elderly gentleman in a deerstalker, for nowadays I climbed in French shorts and an old and tattered lace blouse. I felt hostile eyes boring into my back as we went through the farmyard.

There was little wind that day, and none at all on the west face. On a hot June day time goes slowly, and there was no hurry; we had the whole day and evening before us. We explored at our leisure, wandering across the face towards the high amphitheatre in its centre, up a few pitches of a buttress ("B" Buttress, I think) and along a rake where the unclimbed gullies overhung us—and dropped away below—and into the amphitheatre where strange towers rose out of the sloping scree and we said how impressive it must be in mist. Then, by way of easy gullies, gradually steepening until we had to use the rope, where the sun beat into the dry and stony rifts and Monica (who had been brought up there) said it was as hot as India. I remember, on the last pitches of the last gully, looking up and seeing a tuft of dead grass shaking in the breeze on top, and pointing it out to Monica in encouragement.

It was early afternoon when we came out of the gully. There were nine hours of daylight before us and already the breeze was reviving our parched and sweating bodies.

We moved up slowly to the summit of the Aonach Dubh and then, unwilling to go down with all those grey mountains swimming in the haze around us, we tramped the circuit of the Lost Glen, reversing my walk of the winter, walking through the old snowdrifts to cool our feet, myself remembering the mist and the blizzard and cutting steps down off Stob Coire nan Lochan.

The following day we explored again; this time the steep little cliff on the east side of the Aonach Dubh. The sun still shone in a cloudless sky, and I slept shamelessly after lunch until Monica roused me to climb again. I climbed in a hazy dream until I was brought up short by a hard move, when I reflected ruefully that heat and dryness are no excuse for lack of concentration, and, with an effort, brought my mind back to the rock.

That evening we reached the road without incident and then, suddenly, fatigue overcame us, and we sat down on the bank, desperately in need of a lift to take us the last few miles to the hut. But when the first car stopped and asked if we were going to Kingshouse we said yes spontaneously, and so, an hour and two drinks later, we started the last stage across the moor, staggering a little, drunk with heat and fatigue (not with two beers) and very content.

Monica left for London the next day and I travelled, by easy stages, back to Skye. There was a haze of bluebells in the woods now, and the dream-like quality of the heat wave persisted. I stopped in Fort William to visit Jim Cameron and felt rather guilty, walking into the hospital, very brown and fit and relaxed, and there was Jim, looking rather ill and shaken, in a dressing gown and slippers, listening enviously to my tales of Skye and Glencoe. A rib had pierced his lung but his spine hadn't been damaged, as was thought when he was first admitted to the hospital. Mr. Duff looked tired too; and I felt out of place in Fort William staying just long enough to visit old friends and see the film of Everest which was showing that evening.

I hitched to Mallaig through miles of flaming rhododendrons, and then caught the bus from Armadale to Broadford where every wood and field was drenched with bluebells—and I met a man at Broadford who had known Collie, Mallory, Irvine and Odell and talked about the old days with a nostalgia that had me almost in tears.

There was a lot of mail waiting for me at the youth hostel, among it a letter from Johnnie saying he was in hospital in Yorkshire with a broken back. He had gone to his parents' home on leave and decided to test—or stretch—an old hemp rope by abseiling on it out of a bedroom window. He put the rope round a bed and leaned out of the window horizontally with his feet on the ledge. The last thing he remembered was seeing the bed move towards him across the floor. Then he was lying on his back on the rockery. He said he would probably be fit for the Alps.

Dazed and appalled, I took the letter to a German doctor who was staying at the hostel and he assured me that a squashed vertebra was not too bad, that Johnnie wouldn't be a permanent cripple. I felt a little better and wrote fourteen pages to him before I went to bed, swearing mildly in my relief that it hadn't been worse, feeling all the time the horror of that moment when the bed started to move across the floor.

There was never any monotony in our lives.

The heat wave passed but the weather stayed dry for the first course. This was a Beginners' and we were to make a film for the Mountaineering Association. The cameraman was Norman Keep, the M.A. treasurer. I had four beginners, two of whom, a Lyons Corner House under-manager called Paul, and an Italian countess, Dorothea Gravina, were already competent on rock. The other two, George and Mary, had no experience. I approached this course with some trepidation. I had heard guides say they wouldn't take Beginners' courses on Skye for higher wages than I was getting—and others said they wouldn't take Beginners' courses under any circumstances. The Cuillin are not suitable for parties of novices with one leader. The climbs are long and difficult to escape from in an emergency: too long to have more than two novice behind you. And if I climbed with two only, I was committed to sending the others for a walk, and "walks" on the Cuillin are scrambles of a high standard.

The first day I played safe and taught rope work on the boulders in Coire Lagan. With the hope that something had been learnt, I took two of them on the long and easy Amphitheatre Arête in the afternoon, leaving the others, under the leadership of Norman, to traverse the skyline of Coire Lagan. Two people fell off that day and one retreated from Sgurr Thearlaich with an attack of nerves. People falling off was a secondary consideration, since they were roped and with me, but nerves on the ridge was worrying. I decided to keep the party together in future.

The following day the course went into Coire na Banachdich where a fine sweep of rock ran up to the main ridge. We split into two parties, with Paul and Dorothea leading through on a route parallel to mine, following a line which I picked out as we climbed—a very moderate route, well within their limit. I had George and Mary on my rope, and Norman filmed us from an easy gully.

Roped, we went well. It was when we took the rope off that we had trouble. We were coming down the Sron Dearg ridge of Sgurr Dearg, a blunt edge, not particularly exposed, and broad enough to walk along without using our hands. I had the most competent people in front and bringing up the rear. I was in the middle with Mary in front of me and George directly behind. Suddenly aware that the footsteps behind had stopped, I turned and saw George, very white, standing motionless on the crest. He was quite unable to move. (How long had he been looking at the drop and calculating how far he would fall when he slipped?) He stared at me miserably.

The whole caravan had stopped. Quietly I told him to come on, but he couldn't move. I uncoiled the rope and gave him an end. He muttered something about it being no use.

I said confidently, "If you come off, I shall jump over the other side."

He said nothing, but when I moved on, carrying coils, he followed, and we had no more bad moments that day.

Such situations, although saved, were very shattering to the one who had the responsibility, and by the last morning I was getting ready to breathe a hefty sigh of relief that the course was over. But Norman wanted to film me climbing, and abseiling off, the Inaccessible Pinnacle. To reach it I gave them one last ridge walk: up Coire na Dorus and over Ghreadaidh and Banachdich. Coming down Sgurr Ghreadaidh the order was the same as it had been on Sron Dearg. I was ignoring the first three, giving all my attention to George who was coming down a steep section of the knife-edge to the level part where I was standing. Below, the cliffs dropped away on either side. Unlike Sron Dearg, this *was* exposed. Paul and Dorothea had continued past the level section and were about a hundred feet ahead. By a coincidence I looked away from George for a moment, and saw Dorothea leaping back towards me with her arms outstretched and a terrified look on her face. I shouted to the last men to stay where they were—and then I don't remember moving, but it must have been fast because I heard the rocks falling as I scattered the rotten crest off the ridge. When I reached Dorothea, Mary was scrambling back on to the ridge, where she sat down, trembling a little and speechless, her face completely drained of colour.

Fortunately she kept up a running commentary on all her movements and, being a parson's daughter, "Oh dear," in sepulchral tones, meant she was at the end of her tether. Dorothea, hearing this, coupled with the sound of a slip, had turned to see Mary clinging to her last handhold. She had raced back, wedged a shoulder and foot under the girl, and levered her back on to the ridge.

I stood there, breathing hard and staring at them. We all looked about a hundred years old. Then I went back for Norman and George.

The day ended with Dorothea and me performing for the film on the Pinnacle. The course ended with my asking Norman—as an officer of the Mountaineering Association—to recommend that, after this season, no more Beginners' courses should be held on Skye.

During the month that followed I began to feel tired. The bad weather continued and often I was soaked to the skin. I was living in my tent again. Sometimes I managed to dry my clothes at the Holiday Fellowship centre where my students stayed, but often they were damp in the morning. My sleeping bag was never dry. I had no lilo and my groundsheet was starting to tear in places. The field I had camped in previously was under hay, so I found another camp site behind Wall End farm. Unfortunately the only place that I could find which was sheltered from the south-west gales was in one corner, and close to a stream. I watched that stream as it rose a little more every day—and listened to it at night. I wasn't sleeping well, and found it hard to get up in the morning. I didn't feel like cooking when I came home at night, and I lived on a diet of bread and cheese and apples.

The weather was freakish, often clearing on the off-days, so that, taking advantage of it, I climbed with friends instead of relaxing, with the result that I never had an off-day and I became nervous and frightened.

One day, on Crescent Climb: a very easy Moderate on Pavey, I was halfway up, with a lot of rope behind me, and I paused at a place where I had never hesitated before. I pawed at the rock, tried to left and right, and came back to stare hopelessly at the next easy move. I looked down at my second—and at the screes beyond him—and knew that I was very frightened. I went up, but I was trembling when I reached the stance.

I was very, very tired, and the worse I felt, the less I ate. I was caught up in a vicious circle, and very soon I was going to the Alps.

Then one night the stream rose and water seeped through the bank, and my sleeping bag was a sodden mass of feathers. The following day, after bread and butter for breakfast, I managed one climb on Scout Crag before the rain drove us back to the Holiday Fellowship and lectures. That evening, returning late to the tent, I startled a cow who had her head under the canvas. She jumped, and one horn ripped the tent from top to bottom.

I slept very little that night in the wet bag and in the morning I gave up the struggle. There were three days left of the course, three days before I was due for the Alps. Sid Cross and his wife welcomed me at the Old Dungeon Ghyll with open arms. Everyone else had been washed out of their tents; there was no room in the hotel, but that night I slept on a camp bed in the bar.

Next day I moved into the hotel proper. It was pure bliss to eat like a civilised human being again. It was roast beef that first night (roast pork and roast chicken the following nights) and there was a Swiss waiter who came round and asked me if I wanted more. And after everyone had left the dining-room I was still helping myself to biscuits and cheese from the sideboard.

I washed all my clothes and dried everything on the hot water tanks. I bathed and slept in clean sheets in a dry bed. I had enormous packed lunches to take out with me, and, although we did no spectacular climbs, those last three days became, overnight, a holiday, and—when Johnnie arrived on the last night—I was straining at the leash at the thought of the Alps.

«The whole splendour of our situation»

Elizabeth Stark
and the First Women's Himalayan Expedition, 1955

By 1955, several women had gained climbing experience in the Himalaya, the highest mountains on earth. Fanny Bullock Workman had been doing so since the turn of the century; Hettie Dyhrenfurth had climbed 24,000-foot Sia Kangri in 1934; and Claude Kogan, who is still regarded as one of the greatest mountaineers of all time, reached 23,410-foot Nun in 1953 and climbed a year later to approximately 25,000 feet on Cho Oyu. But there had as yet been no Himalayan expeditions composed exclusively of women. The situation was like that faced by Miriam O'Brien in the 1920s: much of the challenge and satisfaction of Himalayan climbing derived from actually organizing and leading an expedition, but women could never have that experience if they climbed only as occasional members of otherwise male parties.

The Himalayan equivalent of the *cordée féminine* was the women-only expedition, the first of which was organized by four members of the Ladies' Scottish Climbing Club—Evelyn Camrass, Esmé Speakman, Monica Jackson, and Elizabeth Stark. Jackson wrote afterward, perhaps rather disingenuously, that it was "not until our plans had begun to take shape that it occurred to us that we were creating a precedent," adding that "when we realised that we would be pioneering in more senses than one, we were quite pleased, since it seemed to us that this might improve our chances of obtaining financial backing. On the other hand, we thought it would mean that we would have

to contend with a good deal of prejudice at first. Both these sur-
mises proved correct." The group received financial backing
from newspapers interested in covering such an unusual "first"
and from various equipment manufacturers who supplied gear.
These donations were helpful but not sufficient; the climbers
each wound up scrambling to buy their own used equipment at
cut-rate prices and had to take out personal loans in order to
make the trip at all. They were not funded by either the Royal
Geographical Society or the Alpine Club, groups that probably
would have supported the climbers had they been men.

When the women applied for their permit to travel through
Nepal, they encountered prejudice in the form of anxious British officials who, as Jackson put it, thought they "would never
reach the mountains at all but be murdered, robbed or raped by
brigands on the way." Others felt they would be able to "travel
with perfect safety among the friendly people of the foothills,
but thought we should certainly come to grief among the mountains themselves." The officials were finally convinced that the
women had the requisite experience traveling and climbing in
the Himalaya, but nonetheless refused to approve their plans
without "*a further very strong recommendation. Our mountaineer-*
ing experience was all very well, but what, it was asked, would
we do with a drunken Sherpa?" The women knew that Sherpas
could be depended on to behave better than most European
men, and it is perhaps ironic that the permit was not approved
until Jackson revealed how she had once "hitch-hiked to the
Alps with another girl, coping *en route* with Communist lorry-
drivers, an emotional attorney and a traveling circus."

The area they had chosen to explore was the Jugal Himal,
a cluster of peaks rising beyond the Nepali village of Tempathang to heights of nearly twenty-three thousand feet. The
fringes of this region had been glimpsed earlier by H. W. Til-
man, but the Jugal Himal remained a blank on the map, "the
last great unexplored area in Nepal," so inaccessible as to be
unvisited even by the local people. Speakman became ill at
the last minute and dropped out of the expedition, leaving the
other three women the challenge of discovering a route from
Tempathang to the Jugal glaciers and from there, they hoped,
up at least one of the high peaks. They eventually succeeded
in both objectives, climbing a 22,000-foot summit they named

Gyalgen Peak in honor of their Nepali *sirdar,* or foreman,
Mingma Gyalgen.

The excerpt below, written by Stark and reprinted from her
and Monica Jackson's book *Tents in the Clouds,* describes the
middle stages of the expedition. It is not about reaching a summit but about some of the less spectacular aspects of Himalayan
climbing, about life lived in contact with a genuinely different
culture and in a new and strangely beautiful environment—
about teamwork, relationship, and discovery.

WE NOW HAD a day of rest but, as usually happens, it was busier than
many of our climbing days.

We paid off the Tempathang men, all but two, Nima Lama and a
lively youth, Lakpa. These two stayed to help carry loads to the edge of
the glacier, and to fetch up some of their fellows when we were ready
to return to Kathmandu. Mingma had difficulty in persuading any of
them to stay, and eventually, without consulting us, offered full pay for
the time spent at base. We made a fuss about this, though we honoured
his promises. We were always out to correct the misapprehension
which is so common nowadays, that expeditions have money to burn.
The Sherpas, for instance, were strictly honest but this did not prevent
them from trying to get the last anna out of us by any means they
considered legitimate. The general impression seemed to be that we
would never miss it.

Before they left, Monica persuaded the Tempathang men into a
group to be photographed. They lost all their liveliness and posed as
stiff and formal as a Victorian family group. Couldn't they laugh, she
asked? The question struck them as so delightfully absurd they burst
into loud and hearty guffaws, rolling on the ground, and it was a long
time before they could be persuaded to stop.

Next morning, 24th April, we reached the crest of the grassy spur,
which Evelyn had rounded with Mingma. The moraine of the Phurbi
Chyachumbu glacier was far below, a mass of snow-upholstered boulders bordering gritty ice, on neither of which it seemed likely we
should find a comfortable couch. Nor did it seem half so easy to reach
this unattractive spot as Evelyn had talked us into imagining. On the
descent we should have to move leftward and cross two deep gullies,
snow-filled, but banked on either side with mud and scree, like slag

heaps in consistency. In the first of these the snow was ominously lined with brown—the tracks of falling stones. Half-way across, a small avalanche had bared a slope of frozen mud, some boulders stuck in it as impermanently as raisins in a dumpling. On these we crossed, kicking away the looser stuff. Ang Droma had difficulty with a carelessly-bound load of firewood, which she had collected on the way. She would only cross when Evelyn, moving backwards, held her hand, but Murari was very quick and sure-footed, supported only by my black umbrella.

It surprised us, therefore, when he announced he was going back, the more so since he had been eager to accompany us that morning. We told him to stay where he was till Ang Droma and the porters returned.

The snow came on at this point, much earlier than the day before. We did not realise it yet, but a monsoon current was setting in, bringing with it a routine of afternoon cloud and snow. During the march we had been able to see the peaks clearly all day. Now if we were lucky the clouds held off till 1 P.M., but more often they were up by noon and on the whole, they came earlier each day as time went on. Often this hindered our exploration.

Left behind, Murari became cold and, being city-bred, could not stand the loneliness of the mist for long. Eventually he came as far as the moraine camp, but cared so little for the raw cold and the ugliness of the séracs that he never asked to come again. This was convenient, yet made us sad. He had a sensitive, venturesome spirit and a certain nimbleness, the makings of a good mountaineer, and we did not like to see them going to waste.

The porters had come over the snow bare-foot and with bare hands. Nima Lama pulled down the long woollen sleeves of his shirt, but Lapka, who combined charm with a remarkable sense of theatre, had succeeded in getting Evelyn to lend him a pair of gloves. She now asked him to give them back. An incredulous look came into his eyes, which shortly after appeared to brim with tears. He blew pathetically on those fingers which had begun to protrude from the gloves, and she had not the heart to insist, remembering a second spare pair in her sack. Apparently there was no such word as "lend" in Sherpa.

We decided not to move on that day into bad weather and unknown territory, but in the afternoon it cleared slightly. Since Monica was the fittest, for Evelyn felt a little seedy, too, at this height, she set off with Mingma and Ang Temba to reconnoitre a route through that part of the ice-fall above camp. We watched anxiously as they made their way up through the narrowing corridor of the *bergschrund*, which by-passed the maze of séracs and pinnacles in midstream and led to the upper part of the glacier. This corridor was constantly under the threat of falling stones, which made it highly unsafe, and we had already rejected it as a through route. In the afternoon it sounded as if a pitched battle was going on, some of the stones falling quite near camp and hurling themselves savagely on everything in their path as if angry at being displaced. Evelyn and I were relieved to see the others find a way out, up on to the ice itself. We caught sight of them only occasionally after that, creeping over huge snow-covered blocks or perched on spires of ice.

To Monica the reconnaissance must have been like a topographical game of snakes and ladders, played out in sober earnest. Now they would make a mistaken trail, leading to an impasse, where a huge black pocket of ice waited as the penalty for a false move. Now they would find the right line and be rewarded by a shining upward-leading crest into the next puzzle. Mingma cut steps with dash and vigour—he was always at his best in a situation of this kind—and Monica followed, cutting intermediate steps, the result exactly fitting her stride. But in spite of the séracs raised in threat above, and the crevasses lurking below, Mingma was reluctant to put on the rope.

This reluctance to rope was the only difficulty we had with our Sherpas. They went where we wanted to go, respecting our judgment, and though Mingma made excellent suggestions as to the route, he left the final decision to us. Mingma and Ang Temba showed more initiative in climbing than the others, Mingma, who is a competent and experienced mountaineer, being especially keen to lead. We did not discourage them because it was better to share the work of trail-breaking and step-cutting with the Sherpas, whose strength, obviously, was greater than ours. They identified themselves more closely with our project as a result. They did not think it odd that women should be tackling this kind of thing, for their own women, though they do not climb on snow and ice, are tough and adventurous. Sherpas are not dominated by their own women, however, and tactless management of them on our part would have been disastrous.

We were glad that Mingma and Ang Temba had something of the true spirit of mountaineering and a love of adventure, even though these were allied to a blithe disregard for objective danger (except stone-fall which they treated with great respect). So far few Sherpas have wanted to climb mountains for their own sake, and none have planned an expedition on their own account. Tenzing, of course, is a notable exception and others will follow him. Eventually the Sherpas may become guides and leaders, in the same way as Swiss guides, climbing better than amateurs, evolved from the Swiss porter-peasant of the mid-nineteenth century. As yet Sherpas know little of map and compass work or of mountain rescue, but already a school of mountaineering has been opened for them in Darjeeling.

The rope was put on, and Mingma perfunctorily showed Ang Temba how to belay. Ang Temba drove his axe into an inch or two of snow, which would never have held in case of a fall. Such behaviour made the rope more of a danger than a safeguard and several times Monica had to insist on a better belay. "*Thik hai*, memsahib," Ang Temba would say light-heartedly, meaning that everything was fine. The only cure for him, we thought, was to fall right into a crevasse— but we had no wish for it to be administered in the course of our expedition.

They reached the almost level stretch of the glacier above before returning. Monica came back to the tent and overwhelmed us with enthusiasm and snow.

"Look, there's a simply splendid route through the ice-fall," she said. "We'll be able to go right up this glacier." Mingma hovered outside to have some part in bringing the good news, and all we could see of him was a huge grin, like the Cheshire cat's.

Each morning had the same quality of excitement about it in our high camps; a quality which did not necessarily hale us out of our sleeping-bags, but—this was its special attraction—which could be savoured in anticipation and in comfort. We never could tell what we would find on looking out; what new unclimbed, unnamed mountains would have taken shape in the mists of the previous day's advance, or what new and perhaps terrible aspects of the mountains we had already seen would have appeared to shock and humble us. If I had ever entertained any ideas of "proving myself" against these mountains, I lost them now for good.

The sun reached us earlier this morning and the snow, spread everywhere unwrinkled, was beaded and sparkling. We got off to a good start, though Evelyn was suddenly sick in the snow. The Sherpas murmured sympathetically and with unfailing courtesy averted their eyes and made no fuss. The worst of this sickness was that it made her feel no better afterwards. She kept going, however, slowly and with valiant effort, stopping often to clean her goggles which had steamed, and often cleaning her goggles in order to stop.

Though I felt sympathy for her, I could not conceal my excitement. We were crossing a narrow neck at the head of the lower part of the glacier, which then opened out into a huge white horse-shoe, surrounded by magnificent peaks and their attendant glaciers, each poised over the central one in a lingering fall. No one had ever been here or seen all this before.

It is impossible for most human beings to sustain for long such feelings as we now experienced and much of our time and attention in this splendid horse-shoe, unrivalled by anything in our imagination, was taken up with mundane, trivial things. Yet the thought of these trivial things—the way Ang Temba carried his axe upside down, for instance, making patterns in the snow for fun, recalls in a moment the whole splendour of our situation, and all the wonder and joy we felt in it.

Selected Bibliography

Adams, B. S. "Would a Girl Guide Keep You Climbing?" *Illustrated World* 38 (December, 1922): 548–49, 632. About Alma Wagen, an early professional guide on Mount Rainier.

Allison, Stacy. "Thoughts about Everest." *American Alpine Journal* 31 (1989): 18–21. Allison was the first American woman to climb Mount Everest.

Allison, Stacy, and Peter Carlin. *Beyond the Limits: A Woman's Triumph on Everest.* New York: Little, Brown, 1993.

Amann, Hans. "La Fiancée du Mont Blanc." *Les Alpes* 65 (January–March, 1989): 19–22. About Henriette d'Angeville.

Ament, Pat. "Beauty among the Bolts." *Climbing Art* 5 (July, 1987): 10–15. Interview with top Italian rock climbers Louisa Iovane and Heinz Mariacher.

Angell, Shirley. *Pinnacle Club: A History of Women Climbing.* Glasgow: Pinnacle Club, 1988. Limited to Pinnacle Club members, but still provides useful information on British women's climbing since the 1920s.

Arthur, Elizabeth. *Beyond the Mountain.* New York: Harper & Row, 1983. Fiction set against the backdrop of a women's Himalayan expedition.

Bell, Gertrude Lowthian. *The Letters of Gertrude Bell, Selected and Edited by Lady Bell.* New York: Boni and Liveright, 1927.

Benson, Claude Ernest. *British Mountaineering.* London: Routledge, 1914. Includes the chapter "Mountaineering for Ladies."

Bird, Isabella. *A Lady's Life in the Rocky Mountains.* London: John Murray, 1879. Reprint. Norman: University of Oklahoma, 1960; London: Folio Society, 1988.

Birkett, Bill, and Bill Peascod. *Women Climbing: 200 Years of Achievement.* Seattle: Mountaineers, 1990. This and Cicely Williams's *Women on the Rope* are currently the only attempts at a comprehensive history of women in climbing.

Birkett, Dea. *Spinsters Abroad: Victorian Lady Explorers*. London: Gollancz, 1991. Information on Gertrude Bell, Isabella Bird, Fanny Bullock Workman (who was no spinster), and Mary Kingsley.

Blum, Arlene. *Annapurna: A Woman's Place*. San Francisco: Sierra Club, 1980. One of the best expedition books ever written.

_____. "Triumph and Tragedy on Annapurna: Ten Women Challenge Earth's Tenth Highest Mountain." *National Geographic* 155 (March, 1979): 295–311. Widely read article about the 1978 American women's expedition.

Bremer-Kamp, Cherie. *Living on the Edge*. Layton, Utah: Gibbs M. Smith, 1987. Story of the winter attempt on Kangchenjunga that cost Bremer-Kamp's partner, Chris Chandler, his life.

Briglia, Diane. "Back from Beyond." *Climbing* 103 (August, 1987): 63–68. A profile of Cherie Bremer-Kamp.

Bristow, Lily. "An Easy Day for a Lady." *Alpine Journal* 53 (1941–42): 370–74.

Buckingham, J. S. *Belgium, the Rhine, Switzerland, and Holland: An Autumnal Tour, Vol. II.* London: Peter Jackson, Late Fisher, Son, & Co., 1848. Includes an early but secondhand account of d'Angeville's Mont Blanc climb.

Byles, Marie Beuzeville. *By Cargo Boat and Mountain: The Unconventional Experiences of a Woman on Tramp Round the World*. Philadelphia: Lippincott, 1931. Byles climbed New Zealand's Mount Cook, Canada's Mount Assiniboine, and several peaks on the Isle of Skye.

Campbell, Olwen. *Mary Kingsley: A Victorian in the Jungle*. London: Methuen, 1957.

Chorley, Katherine C. *Hills and Highways*. New York: Dutton, 1928. Chorley was evidently a climber, but this book contains only occasional references to the sport.

Clark, Ronald William. *The Early Alpine Guides*. London: Phoenix House, 1949.

_____. *An Eccentric in the Alps: The Story of the Rev. W. A. B. Coolidge.* London: Museum, 1959. Information on Coolidge's aunt, Meta Brevoort.

_____. *The Victorian Mountaineers*. London: Batsford, 1953.

Cobb, Sue. *The Edge of Everest: A Woman Challenges the Mountain*. Harrisburg: Stackpole, 1989.

Cogan, Frances B. *All-American Girl: The Ideal of Real Womanhood in Mid-Nineteenth Century America*. Athens: University of Georgia Press, 1989.

Cole, Mrs. Henry Warwick. *A Lady's Tour Round Monte Rosa; with Visits to the Italian Valleys . . . in the Years 1850–56–58*. London: Longman, Brown, Green, Longman and Roberts, 1859.

Coolidge, W. A. B. [Marguerite "Meta" Brevoort]. "A Day and a Night on the Bietschhorn." *Alpine Journal* 6 (1872): 114–24.

Corcelle, J. Mlle. *Henriette d'Angeville. Une Ascension célèbre au Mont-Blanc (1838)*. Bourg: Courrier de l'Ain, 1900.

Corning, Ursula. "Space below My Feet." Review in *American Alpine Journal* 13 (1962–63): 306–307.

————. "A Woman's Reach." Review in *American Alpine Journal* 16 (1968–69): 485–86.

Cowles, Elizabeth. "More about the Santa Marta." *American Alpine Journal* 4 (1942): 362–68. Climbing in a little-known range in South America.

Craig, Robert W. *Storm and Sorrow in the High Pamirs*. Seattle: Mountaineers, 1977. Information about the Soviet attempt on Peak Lenin in which Elvira Shatayeva and seven other women died.

Crawford, Mary E. "Mountain Climbing for Women." *Canadian Alpine Journal* 2 (1909): 85–91.

Curran, Jim. *K2: Triumph and Tragedy*. Seattle: Mountaineers, 1987. Information concerning Julie Tullis's last climb.

d'Angeville, Henriette. "A Letter to Markham Sherwill." In *Mont Blanc: An Anthology*, edited by Claire Eliane Engel, 110–11. New York: Rand McNally, 1965.

————. *Mon Excursion au Mont-Blanc en 1838*. Paris: Arthaud, 1987.

d'Arve, Stéphen [Edmund de Catelin]. *Histoire du Mont Blanc et de la Vallée de Chamonix*. Paris: Delagrave, 1879. Information on Henriette d'Angeville.

da Silva, Rachel, ed. *Leading Out: Women Climbers Reaching for the Top*. Seattle: Seal Press, 1992. A collection of mostly contemporary writings by climbers such as Alison Osius, Louise Shepherd, Susan Edwards, and Wendy Roberts.

De Watteville, Vivienne. *Speak to the Earth: Wanderings and Reflections among Elephants and Mountains*. Preface by Edith Wharton. London: Methuen, 1935. Includes a chapter on the author's brief encounter with Mount Kenya.

Deacock, Antonia. *No Purdah in Padam: The Story of the Women's Overland Himalayan Expedition, 1958*. London: Harrap, 1960.

Dingle, Graeme. *Two Against the Alps*. Christchurch, New Zealand: Whitcombe and Tombs, 1972. The author and Jill Tremaine made the first winter traverse of the New Zealand Alps.

Du Faur, Freda. *The Conquest of Mount Cook and Other Climbs: An Account of Four Seasons' Mountaineering in the Southern Alps of New Zealand.* London: George Allen & Unwin, 1915.

Dundas, Anne Louise. *Beneath African Glaciers: The Humors, Tragedies and Demands of an East African Government Station as Experienced by an Official's Wife.* London: H. F. & G. Witherby, 1924. Dundas climbed to 15,200 feet on Kilimanjaro, but the men in her party refused to let her go higher.

Dunsheath, Joyce. *Guest of the Soviets: Moscow and the Caucasus 1957.* London: Constable, 1959.

_____. *Mountains and Memsahibs.* London: Constable, 1958.

_____. "Mrigthuni, Garhwal." *American Alpine Journal* 14 (1965): 472.

Dunsheath, Joyce, and Eleanor Bailey. *Afghan Quest.* London: Harrap, 1961.

Dyhrenfurth, Hettie. *Memsahib in Himalaya.* Leipzig: Verlag Deutsche Buchwerkstätten, 1931.

Edwards, Amelia Ann Blanford. *Untrodden Peaks and Unfrequented Valleys: A Midsummer Ramble in the Dolomites.* London: Longman's, 1873. Reprint. London: Virago, 1986.

Engel, Claire Eliane. "Early Lady Climbers." *Alpine Journal* 54 (1943–44): 51–59. Concerns treatment of women mountaineers in fiction.

_____. *A History of Mountaineering in the Alps.* London: Allen & Unwin, 1950.

_____. *Mountaineering in the Alps: An Historical Survey.* London: Allen & Unwin, 1971.

_____. *They Came to the Hills.* London: George Allen & Unwin, 1952. Information on Lucy Walker and Elizabeth Le Blond.

Engelhard, Georgia. "Challenge of High Places." *Christian Science Monitor Monthly Magazine* (June 30, 1937): 6.

_____. "High Up on Teton Peaks." *American Photography* 43 (January, 1949): 28–32.

_____. *Peterli and the Mountain.* Philadelphia: Lippincott, 1954.

_____. "Switzerland's Enchanted Val d'Hérens." *National Geographic* 107 (June, 1955): 825–48.

Farrar, J. P. "In Memoriam: Mrs. Fanny Bullock Workman." *Alpine Journal* (1925): 180–82.

Frank, Katherine. *A Voyager Out: The Life of Mary Kingsley.* Boston: Houghton Mifflin, 1986.

Freer, Catherine. "Cholatse North Face." *Climbing* 89 (April, 1985): 38–42. Himalayan climbing by one of the best climbers of the 1980s.

Freshfield, Mrs. Henry. *Alpine Byways, or, Light Leaves Gathered in 1859 and 1860*. London: Longman, Green, Longman, and Roberts, 1861.

————. *A Summer Tour in the Grisons and the Italian Valleys of the Bernina*. London: Longman, Green, Longman, and Roberts, 1862.

Fuller, Fay. "A Trip to the Summit." *Every Sunday*, August 23, 1890. Reprinted in *Island in the Sky: Pioneering Accounts of Mount Rainier, 1833–1894*, edited by Paul Schullery, 125–40. Seattle: Mountaineers, 1987.

Gaillard, Emile. *Une ascension romantique en 1838: Henriette d'Angeville au Mont-Blanc*. Chambéry: Editions Lire, 1947.

Gardiner, Frederick, and Charles Pilkington. "In Memoriam: Miss Lucy Walker." *Alpine Journal* 31 (February, 1917): 98.

Gardiner, Steve. *Why I Climb: Personal Insights of Top Climbers*. Harrisburg: Stackpole, 1990. Includes profiles of Jann Conn, Arlene Blum, Beverly Johnson, Alison Osius, and Lynn Hill.

Geiger, William A. "Dorothea [sic] and I. A. Richards on Mountaineering." In *Essays on the Literature of Mountaineering*, edited by Armand E. Singer. Morgantown: West Virginia University Press, 1982. Includes a discussion of Dorothy Pilley's *Climbing Days*, 81–86.

Goodman, Susan. *Gertrude Bell*. Dover, N.H.: Berg, 1985.

Gos, Charles. *Près de Névés et des Glaciers: Impressions Alpestres*. 5th ed. Paris: Fischbacher, n.d. Information on Henriette d'Angeville.

Greenwood, Sallie. "Frame of Reference: A Historical Perspective." *Climbing* 103 (August, 1987): 44–46. Well-informed discussion of women's climbing.

Greer, Barry. "Connubial Climbing." *Summit: A Mountaineering Magazine* 32 (September–October, 1986): 26–28. A look at how climbers of both sexes attempt to balance climbing, marriage, and family.

Gribble, Francis Henry. *The Early Mountaineers*. London: T. Fisher Unwin, 1899. Includes a chapter on the "First Lady Mountaineers."

Grissom, Kitty Calhoun. "A Himalayan Classic—Makalu's West Pillar." *American Alpine Journal* 33 (1991): 7–13.

Hamilton, Helen. *Mountain Madness*. London: W. Collins, 1922. Climbs in the Alps. Hamilton records this exchange with a local guide: "Once I asked him, knowing his absolute candour, whether guides considered climbing with women to be more dangerous to them than climbing with men. After some consideration he replied that, generally speaking, they preferred *patrons* of their own sex. Women, he said, though often more sure of foot and balance than men, and less clumsy, are apt to get suddenly exhausted, or to lose their nerve.

When, however, they are reliable in these respects, they are the more desirable companions, inasmuch as they are less given to arguing with their guides, and go, as a rule, unmurmuring where they are led" (191).

Harper, Stephen. *Lady Killer Peak: A Lone Man's Story of Twelve Women on a Killer Mountain.* London: World Distributors, 1965. Misogynistic and condescending account of the 1959 Cho Oyu expedition on which Claude Kogan died.

Healy, Trudy. *From the Black Mountain to Tibet: One Woman's Mountains.* New York: Vantage Press, 1993.

Hechtel, Sibylle. "Untitled." *American Alpine Journal* (1974). Hechtel wanted to title this report on the first *cordée féminine* ascent of El Capitan "Walls without Balls," but the *AAJ* editorial board preferred a title, "Keeping Abreast of El Cap," that punned on female rather than male anatomy. The essay appeared as "Untitled." A more recent version was published as "Walls without Balls" in *Rock and Roses,* edited by Mikel Vause, 61–70.

Higgins, Molly. "First Time." In *Yosemite Climber,* edited by George Meyers, 54–63. London: Diadem, 1979. The first *cordée féminine* ascent of El Capitan by the famous Nose route.

Hobson, Alan, and John Amatt. *One Step Beyond: Rediscovering the Adventure Attitude.* Banff, Alberta: Altitude Publishing, 1992. Includes information on Laurie Skreslet and Sharon Wood, who climbed Everest.

Holland, T. H. "Mountaineering in the North-West Himalaya." *Nature* 84 (July 21, 1910): 78–80. Review of the Workmans' *Peaks and Glaciers of Nun Kun.*

Holmes, Julia Archibald. *A Bloomer Girl on Pike's Peak, 1858.* Edited by Agnes Wright Spring. Denver: Denver Public Library Western History Department, 1949.

Hornby, Emily. *Mountaineering Records.* Liverpool: J. A. Thompson, 1907.

"In the Ice World of the Himalaya." Review in *Athenaeum* 2 (November 3, 1900): 570.

Jackson, Eileen Montague. *Switzerland Calling: A True Tale of a Boy and Girl's Wonderful Summer Holidays Climbing in the Alps.* London: A. & C. Black, 1927.

Jackson, Monica. *The Turkish Time Machine.* London: Hodder, 1966.

————. "The Woman Climber." In *The Book of Modern Mountaineering,* edited by Malcolm Milne, 258–66. New York: G. P. Putnam's Sons, 1968.

Jackson, Monica, and Elizabeth Stark. *Tents in the Clouds: The First Women's Himalayan Expedition.* London: Travel Book Club, 1957.

Jackson, Mrs. E. P. "A Winter Quartette." *Alpine Journal* 14 (February, 1889): 200–10.

Jones, Chris. *Climbing in North America.* Berkeley: University of California Press, 1976. The only "comprehensive" history of American climbing; only a few paragraphs devoted to women.

Keen, Dora. "Arctic Mountaineering by a Woman." *Scribner's Monthly* 52 (July, 1912): 64–80.

————. "Climbing the Giant's Tooth." *Scribner's Monthly* 60 (October, 1916): 427–38.

————. "How I Climbed a 14,000-Foot Mountain." *Ladies' Home Journal* 30 (August, 1913): 7, 41.

————. "Woman's Ascent of the Matterhorn." *Outlook* 95 (May 28, 1910): 206–13.

————. "Woman's Climb in the High Alps." *National Geographic* 22 (July, 1911): 642–75.

Kelly, Emily. "The Pinnacle Club." *Journal of the Fell and Rock Climbing Club of the English Lake District* 5 (1919–21): 324–26.

Kingsley, Mary Henrietta. *The Ascent of Cameroon's Peak and Travels in French Congo.* Liverpool: "Journal of Commerce" Printing Works, 1896.

Knowlton, Elizabeth. *The Naked Mountain.* New York: G. P. Putnam's Sons, 1933. Knowlton participated in an early attempt on Nanga Parbat, but didn't climb high.

————. "Petite Première in the Mont Blanc Massif." *Atlantic* 146 (September, 1930): 354–65.

————. "Rock-Climbing in Skye." *American Alpine Journal* 5 (1943–45): 373–78.

Kogan, Claude, and Raymond Lambert. *White Fury: Gaurisankar and Cho Oyu.* Translated by Showell Styles. London: Hurst & Blackett, 1956.

L., E. C. "Mountain Climbing for Women." *Country Life in America* 20 (June 1, 1911): 20.

Ladies' Alpine Club Journal (title varies: *Ladies' Alpine Club Report, Yearbook,* etc.). London. 1907–75.

Ladies' Scottish Climbing Club Journal. Falkirk, Scotland. 1929– .

Le Blond, Elizabeth. *Adventures on the Roof of the World.* New York: Dutton, 1904.

————. *Day In, Day Out.* London: Bodley Head, 1928. Le Blond's autobiography.

————. *The High Alps in Winter: Or, Mountaineering for Health.* London: Sampson Low, 1883.

————. *High Life and Towers of Silence*. London: Sampson Low, 1886.

————. *Mountaineering in the Land of the Midnight Sun*. London: T. Fisher Unwin, 1908.

————. *My Home in the Alps*. London: Sampson Low, 1892.

————. "Perils of the High Peaks." *Cosmopolitan* 37 (July, 1904): 245–52.

————. *True Tales of Mountain Adventure for Non-climbers Young and Old*. London: T. Fisher Unwin, 1902.

Lefebure, Molly. *Scratch & Co.: The Great Cat Expedition*. New York: Meredith Press, 1969. A "young adult" book, but a great read for adults as well, a delightful story as well as a keen satire on the nationalism and racism of the early Himalayan expeditions. A team of cats—all Toms, I'm afraid—attempts to climb HKP, "Highest Known Peak," using rabbits as porters and sturdy little terriers as "Sherpas." The redoubtable team advances steadily upward, until the foxes show up. . . .

Leininger, Nicole, and Georges Kogan. *The Ascent of Alpamayo: An Account of the Franco-Belgian Expedition to the Cordillera Blanca in the High Andes*. New York: J. de Graff, 1954.

Lunn, Arnold. *A Century of Mountaineering, 1857–1957*. London: Allen & Unwin, 1957. A comprehensive history published on the hundredth anniversary of the Alpine Club.

————. *Matterhorn Centenary*. London: George Allen & Unwin, 1965. Includes a chapter on Lucy Walker's pioneering ascent of the Matterhorn.

Masson, Bonney. "Ideas—Women and Climbing." *Mountain* 85 (June, 1982): 44.

Matteson, Herman Howard. "How Much of a Coward Are You? A Woman Mountain Guide Tells of Her Experiences with Fear on the High Ridges." *Sunset* 48 (June, 1922): 36–39. About Alma Wagen, the early professional guide on Mount Rainier.

Mazuchelli, Nina E. *The Indian Alps and How We Crossed Them: Being a True Narrative of Two Years' Residence in the Eastern Himalaya and Two Months' Tour into the Interior*. New York: Dodd, Mead, 1876.

Merriam, Esther. "Women Mountain-Climbers." *Harper's Bazaar* 44 (November, 1910): 634.

Middleton, Dorothy. *Victorian Lady Travellers*. New York: Dutton, 1965.

Moffat, Gwen. *On My Home Ground*. London: Hodder and Stoughton, 1968.

_____. *Space below My Feet*. London: Hodder and Stoughton, 1961.

_____. *Survival Count*. London: Gollancz, 1972.

Morin, Nea. *A Woman's Reach: Mountaineering Memoirs*. New York: Dodd, Mead, 1969.

Müller, Chr[istian]. "Ascent of Mont Blanc, by Mademoiselle d'Angeville." *Colburn's New Monthly Magazine* 160 (1840): 387–91.

Mummery, Mary. "Der Teufelsgrat." In *My Climbs in the Alps and Caucasus*, by Albert Frederick Mummery, 66–95. London: T. F. Unwin, 1896.

Osius, Alison. "Barbara Washburn." *Climbing* 103 (August, 1987): 58–61.

_____. "The Gift." In *Rock and Roses*, edited by Mikel Vause, 99–106. Reprinted in *The Climbing Art* 14 (March, 1990): 2–3.

_____. "In the Labyrinth." *Climbing* 90 (June, 1985): 24–26.

_____. "Karass and Granfalloons." *Ascent* 5 (1989): 87–94.

_____. "The Naked Edge." *Climbing Art* 19 (Summer, 1991): 2–5.

Paillon, Mary. "Mademoiselle d'Angeville: Notice Biographique." *Annuaire du Club Alpin Français* 20 (1893): 401–34.

Peck, Annie Smith. "The First Ascent of Mount Huascaran." *Harper's Monthly Magazine* 118 (January, 1909): 173–87.

_____. "Miss Peck Replies to Mrs. Workman." *Scientific American* 102 (February 16, 1910): 183.

_____. "Practical Mountain Climbing," *Outing* 38 (September, 1901): 695–700.

_____. *A Search for the Apex of America: High Mountain Climbing in Peru and Bolivia*. New York: Dodd, Mead, 1911.

_____. *The South American Tour*. New York: Doran, 1913. Includes a description of Peck's attempt on Sorata.

_____. *Up the Matterhorn. The Perilous Feat of Miss Annie S. Peck*. Newspaper clipping (August 23, 1895) held by Brown University.

People's Physical Culture Publishing House. *Mountaineering in China*. Peking: Foreign Language Press, 1965. Includes the chapters "The Ascent of 'The Father of the Ice Mountains'—China's First Women's World Mountaineering Record" and "The Scaling of Mount Kongur Tiubie Tagh—Another World Record by the Chinese Women's Expedition."

Petzoldt, Patricia. *On Top of the World: My Adventures with My Mountain-Climbing Husband*. New York: Thomas Y. Crowell, 1953.

Piana, Paul. "The Way the Wind Blows." *Climbing* 103 (August, 1987): 76–81. Eulogy for Catherine Freer, an outstanding climber who died on Canada's Mount Logan.

Pierre, Bernard. *La Conquête du Salcantay.* Paris: Dumont, 1953. Claude Kogan was a member of the French team that made the first ascent of this difficult Andean peak.

———. *A Mountain Called Nun Kun.* Translated by Nea Morin and Janet Adam Smith. London: Hodder and Stoughton, 1955. More about Claude Kogan, this time on Nun Kun in the Himalaya.

Pigeon, Anna, and Ellen Abbott. *Peaks and Passes.* London: Griffith Faune, Okeden and Welsh, 1885. Arlene Blum writes that the ascent of the steep southeast side of Monte Rosa by these sisters is "characterized as the first great climbing feat by a woman."

Pilley, Dorothy. *Alps Again.* U.K., n.d. A rare twelve-page pamphlet of Alpine reminiscences, apparently an original publication and not a journal offprint.

———. *Climbing Days.* London: Hogarth, 1989.

———. "Retrospection." Introduction to the second edition of *Climbing Days*, xiii–xxviii. London: Secker & Warburg, 1965.

Pinnacle Club Journal. Midlothian, Scotland. Frequency varies, 1924– .

Plunkett, Frederica Louisa Edith. *Here and There among the Alps.* London: Longmans, Green, 1875.

"Profiles: Eighteen Women Who Climb." *Climbing* 103 (August, 1987): 83–104. Personal insights of contemporary rock climbers.

Reynolds, Jan, and Ned Gillette. *Everest Grand Circle: A Climbing and Skiing Adventure through Nepal and Tibet.* Seattle: Mountaineers, 1985.

Riefenstahl, Leni. *Leni Riefenstahl: A Memoir.* New York: St. Martin's, 1993.

Rizzi, Anne Marie. "Hands." In *The Games Climbers Play,* edited by Ken Wilson, 479–82. San Francisco: Sierra Club, 1978. A rockclimbing partnership goes bad.

Robertson, Janet. *Magnificent Mountain Women.* Lincoln: University of Nebraska Press, 1990. Includes information on Isabella Bird and several other women who climbed in Colorado.

Rogers, Susan. "Finding a Positive History." *Climbing* 103 (August, 1987): 127–29.

Sauvy, Anne. "The Blue Crampon Brigade." In *Mirrors in the Cliffs,* edited by Jim Perrin, 593–602. London: Diadem Books, 1983. Originally published in French in La Montagne (1976).

———. *Flammes de Pierre: Short Stories about Mountains and Mountaineers.* London: Diadem, 1991.

Scarr, Josephine. *Four Miles High.* London: Gollancz, 1966. Women's expedition to Himalaya of India and Nepal.

Schuster, Claud. *Men, Women and Mountains: Days in the Alps and Pyrenees*. London: Nicholson, 1931.

Scot, Barbara. *The Violet Shyness of Their Eyes: Notes from Nepal*. Corvallis, Ore.: Calyx Books, 1993.

Seghers, Carroll. *The Peak Experience: Hiking and Climbing for Women*. Indianapolis: Bobbs Merrill, 1979.

Sharma, Man Mohan. *Of Gods and Glaciers on and around Mt. Rataban*. New Delhi: Vision, 1979. An Indian girls' school climb as described by a man.

Shatayev, Vladimir. *Degrees of Difficulty*. Translated by Deborah Piranian. Seattle: Mountaineers, 1987. Includes a chapter on the women's Peak Lenin attempt that cost Elvira Shatayeva her life.

Smith, Cyndi. *Off the Beaten Track: Women Adventurers and Mountaineers in Western Canada*. Jasper, Alberta: Coyote Books, 1989. Information on such climbers as Lillian Gest, Phyllis James Munday, and Georgia Engelhard.

Smith, Janet Adam. *Mountain Holidays*. London: Travel Book Club, 1946.

Stark, Freya. *The Freya Stark Story*. New York: Coward-McCann, 1953. Includes Stark's earlier book *Traveler's Prelude* (London, 1950), with its occasional references to Stark's climbing in the Alps.

Steiger, John. "Lynn Hill." *Climbing* 103 (August, 1987): 48–57. Profile of one of the world's best contemporary rock climbers.

_____. "So Why Is There a Women's Issue?" *Climbing* 103 (August, 1987): 3.

Stuart-Watt, Eva. *Africa's Dome of Mystery, Comprising the First Descriptive History of the Wachagga People of Kilimanjaro, Their Evangelization, and a Girl's Pioneer Climb to the Crater of Their 19,000 Ft. Snow Shrine*. London: Marshall, Morgan & Scott, 1930. Includes a photo of the frozen leopard made famous in "The Snows of Kilimanjaro."

Tabei, Junko. *Everest Mother*. Tokyo: Shincho-Sha, 1982.

Tejada-Flores, Lito. "Beyond Climbing Games: Alpinism as Humanism— Second Thoughts from Lito Tejada-Flores." *Summit: The Mountain Journal* 36 (Fall, 1990): 25–27.

_____. "The Games Climbers Play." *Ascent* 1 (May, 1967): 23–25.

Thompson, Dorothy Evelyn. *Climbing with Joseph Georges*. Kendal, England: Titus Wilson, 1962.

Tibble, Anne Northgrove. *Gertrude Bell*. London: A&C Black, 1958.

Tuckett, Elizabeth. *How We Spent the Summer: Or a Voyage in Zigzag, in Switzerland and Tyrol, with Some Members of the Alpine Club*. London: Longman's, Greenman's, Green & Co., 1866.

_____. *Zigzagging amongst Dolomites*. London: Longman's, Green, Reader & Dyer, 1871.

Tullis, Julie. *Clouds from Both Sides: An Autobiography by Julie Tullis*. San Francisco: Sierra Club, 1987.

Ullman, James Ramsey. *The Age of Mountaineering*. Philadelphia: J. B. Lippincott, 1954.

Underhill, Miriam (O'Brien). *Give Me the Hills*. London: Methuen, 1956.

Vaucher, Yvette. "Première Féminine de la Face Nord du Cervin." *Les Alpes* (1965): 282–84.

_____. "With Two Men on the Matterhorn." In *Mirrors in the Cliffs*, edited by Jim Perrin, 91–95. London: Diadem, 1983. Originally published in German in *Alpinismus* (1965).

Vause, Mikel. *On Mountains and Mountaineers*. La Crescenta, Calif.: Mountain N'Air Books, 1993. Includes information on Arlene Blum.

Vause, Mikel, ed. *Rock and Roses: An Anthology of Mountaineering Essays*. La Crescenta, Calif.: Mountain N'Air, 1990. Essays by contemporary women climbers, including Arlene Blum, Cherie Bremer-Kamp, Sibylle Hechtel, and Alison Osius.

Visser-Hooft, Jenny. *Among the Kara-Korum Glaciers in 1925*. London: Edward Arnold, 1926. Visser-Hooft, an honorary member of the Dutch Alpine Club, and a (not just honorary) vice-president of the Ladies' Alpine Club, accompanied her husband P. C. Visser in 1925 on the Himalayan survey described in this book.

Vogler, Romain. "The Best Man for This Job May Be a Woman: The New Guiding Tradition in Europe." *Rock and Ice* 26 (July–August, 1988): 26–31.

Wald, Beth. "Reflections." *Climbing* 103 (August, 1987): 70–75.

Waterman, Laura, and Guy Waterman. *Forest and Crag: A History of Hiking, Trail Blazing, and Adventure in the Northeast Mountains*. Boston: Appalachian Mountain Club, 1989.

Williams, Cicely. *Women on the Rope: The Feminine Share of Mountain Adventure*. London: George Allen & Unwin, 1973. A reasonably complete history by an author uncomfortable with feminism.

_____. *Yankee Ice and Rock: A History of Climbing in the Northeastern United States*. Harrisburg, Penn.: Stackpole Books, 1993.

Winstone, Harry Victor Frederick. *Gertrude Bell*. New York: Quartet Books, 1978.

"Women Do an Equal Share with Men." In *Another Ascent of the World's Highest Peak—Qomolangma*. Peking: Foreign Language Press, 1970. A fascinating and unabashedly political account of feminism and alpinism in China.

Workman, Fanny Bullock. "Exploring the Rose." *Independent* 85 (January 10, 1916): 54–56.

_____. "First Ascents of the Hoh Lumba and Sosbon Glaciers in the North West Himalayas." *Independent* 55 (December 31, 1903): 3108–12.

_____. "Miss Peck and Mrs. Workman." *Scientific American* 102 (February 12, 1910): 143.

_____. "Recent First Ascents in the Himalaya." *Independent* 68 (June 2, 1910): 1202–10.

_____. "Woman in the Himalayas." *Putnam's* 7 (January, 1910): 474–82.

Workman, Fanny Bullock, and William Hunter Workman. *The Call of the Snowy Hispar: Narrative of Exploration and Mountaineering on the Northern Frontier of India*. New York: Scribner's, 1911.

_____. *Ice-Bound Heights of the Mustagh: An Account of Two Seasons of Pioneer Exploration and High Climbing in the Baltistan Himalaya*. New York: Scribner's, 1908.

_____. *In the Ice-World of Himalaya: Among the Peaks and Passes of Ladakh, Nubra, Suru, and Baltistan*. New York: Cassell, 1900.

_____. *Peaks and Glaciers of Nun Kun: A Record of Pioneer Exploration and Mountaineering in the Punjab Himalaya*. London: Constable, 1909.

_____. *Two Summers in the Ice-Wilds of Eastern Karakoram: The Exploration of Nineteen Hundred Square Miles of Mountain and Glacier*. London: T. Fisher Unwin, 1917.